THE
vegetarian
RESET

THE
vegetarian
RESET

75 LOW-CARB, PLANT-FORWARD RECIPES from AROUND the WORLD

Vasudha Viswanath

Photographs by Alexandra Shytsman

THE
collective
BOOK STUDIO

For Mira, my three-year-old, who currently rejects all vegetables.

Library of Congress Cataloging in-Publication Data available.
ISBN: 978-1-68555-037-0
Ebook ISBN: 978-1-68555-038-7
Library of Congress Control Number: 2022906998

Printed using Forest Stewardship Council certified stock
from sustainably managed forests.

Manufactured in China.

Editor: Christine McKnight
Design: Liliana Guia
Project Editor: Amy Treadwell.

10 9 8 7 6 5 4 3 2 1

The Collective Book Studio®
Oakland, California
www.thecollectivebook.studio

Contents

Introduction

MY FOOD PHILOSOPHY

The word "vegetarian" evokes two distinct images, depending on whom you ask. Newly turned vegetarians have visions of consuming leafy green salads, smoothies, and perhaps imitation-meat burgers for every meal. Those who have been vegetarian for longer, like me, dream about bread, rice, and noodles. Think about it: When you go out to dinner, omnivores choose between chicken and lamb; vegetarians choose between noodles and fried rice, or between pasta and pizza, with a side salad that's barely worth a mention. White carbs are the focus and vegetables tend to play a supporting role. Recipe books in this space tend to straddle two extremes—they either wax eloquently about how to make the fluffiest focaccia and a garlicky pile of al dente noodles, or on the other hand propose uninspiring combinations of quinoa, greens, and avocado for every meal.

Awareness of our unsustainable food system is driving many to eat more plant-based food. But what is marketed to them is lab-grown burgers, sugary smoothies, and a sensory overload of refined carbs.

With busy and stressful lifestyles, we turn to comfort food whether cooking at home or ordering in. We think exercise will fix everything. But at some point—for me it was after I turned thirty—we all find that we can no longer outrun a bad diet, no matter how many spin classes we take. It is now widely recognized that overconsumption of refined (or processed) carbs—including bread, rice, and pasta—leads to frequent blood sugar spikes and subsequent *insulin resistance*, and is deeply linked to type 2 diabetes, heart disease, obesity, and several other chronic diseases.[*] Excessive starch and sugar create inflammation in our bodies and are highly disruptive to our gut health, hormone regulation, and immune system.

Okay, so refined carbs in large quantities are not good for you. And likely neither is processed imitation meat. But raw salads will not keep your palate happy forever. So how do you make a healthy vegetarian lifestyle satisfying and delicious, and thereby sustainable?

As I thought about this, I narrowed down all my food problems to this simple diagram, a culinary trilemma. How do we find the sweet spot where a healthy vegetarian lifestyle intersects with a foodie's sensibility? This book is the beginning of my humble attempt to solve this puzzle and redefine what it means to be vegetarian. It's time to put the "veg" back in *vegetarian*. It's time to *reset*.

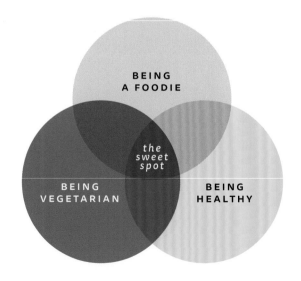

THE CULINARY TRILEMMA OF VEGETARIANISM

* *See appendix for recommended reading*

For inspiration, I turned to the basics. Traditional cuisines of the world have long celebrated vegetables, legumes, and whole grains, using spices and healthy fats liberally and cooking them with techniques that sharpen and amplify their flavors. In this book, I strived to make those ideas accessible and adapt my favorite dishes to put vegetables center stage.

The nutrition-based argument for cutting out processed foods from our diets is clear. In this book, I chose instead to focus on *flavor*. When you embrace *whole foods*, you are transported to a world of heightened flavor where your taste buds don't just appreciate but *relish* a slow-roasted tomato; the mellow but smoky flesh of charred eggplant combined with sweet, caramelized onions; a simple stir-fry where each vegetable is crisp yet just tender enough; or the layers of complexity in a marinated cheese.

If you're a foodie that craves variety, flavor, and adventure, I wrote this book for you. To keep you interested, to keep your palate happy, and to woo you into cooking delicious food that puts nutrition back into focus. I hope these recipes make healthy eating compelling enough that you do it because you *want* to, not just because you should.

THIS BOOK

This book is organized into nine chapters based on the sections you would typically find on a restaurant's menu—Breads, Salads, Soups, Pasta, Desserts, and so on. However, the contents would be extremely atypical of a restaurant's menu! For example, I use riced cauliflower or spiralized vegetables in lieu of white rice or noodles and create breads out of less-processed alternatives like chickpea and almond flour. My desserts are lightly sweetened with whole fruit, as I believe nature intended sugars to be consumed.

Due to their focus on vegetables, the recipes in this book tend to be *moderately low-carb* and are predominantly gluten-free. I've provided nutritional facts for each recipe to empower you to make informed decisions about what you eat. Use them to your advantage when meal-planning. I use a moderate amount of full-fat dairy and eggs in some of my recipes, but often recommend alternatives for people who refrain from animal products.

Do you need to banish refined carbs and sugar from your diet forever? No. However, when you embrace whole foods, you will find that your palate *resets* and your taste buds start to develop a whole new preference. You'll find that after a night out eating junk food, you will crave healthier food for your next meal. Dessert sweetened with refined sugar will begin to taste artificially sweet. My goal is to help you introduce enough healthy meals into your rotation so that you can begin to reset your body in this way.

I hope you enjoy taking this culinary journey with me. Looking back, you'll know you ate well.

About Me

I grew up in Bangalore, India, in a family of foodies where everyone still passionately debates their next meal. My parents fondly recall me, as a three-year-old, demanding to know what was in my lunchbox the night before I went to school. Always an avid and adventurous home cook, some of my favorite childhood memories are of making a pasta with béchamel sauce for my friends and baking cakes in a pressure cooker filled with sand because our oven would not get hot enough for a cake. I have been a lifelong vegetarian, initially from my upbringing and now by choice.

I continued my culinary journey in New York, where I moved to pursue a career on Wall Street at the intersection of technology, finance, and strategy. New York City opened up a whole new world of cuisines and flavors. My husband and I dined out several times a week before our daughter was born, scouring blogs for the best restaurants (the unofficial count is somewhere north of 300). Everything is research. I am the pesky diner that must know what's in every dish and takes notes at dinner. We also traveled extensively and heavily prioritized sampling local cuisine over sightseeing. Travel has been the best teacher, opening our minds and our palates. We took our homework seriously before each trip, researching the local cuisine and its origins, and where we could find the best vegetarian food. When we returned, I would obsessively experiment in my tiny Manhattan kitchen until I perfected my favorite dishes from the trip.

When a routine physical a few months after I had my baby revealed that my hemoglobin A1C was in the pre-diabetic range, I started to research what "healthy" food really meant. I learned that white carbs from starchy foods are broken down almost as fast as sugar in your body—and you can eat a whole lot more pasta than you can eat sugar! I learned that "whole wheat" today usually meant ultra-processed when made in modern mills, and still metabolized quickly to glucose. I learned that I wasn't eating nearly as many vegetables as I was supposed to, and that I didn't need to avoid fat. And I learned about insulin resistance and the science behind why we put on weight.

I began to follow a low-carb, Mediterranean-style diet, cutting down on processed foods, starch, and added sugar. This led me to create alternative versions of the dishes I've enjoyed and that I now present to you. Eating this way has had a transformative effect on my health and energy levels and has become a way of life that is enjoyable and sustainable.

The process of finalizing recipes for this book was exhilarating and excruciating in equal measure. This is the first time I've shared my passion for food and cooking beyond my immediate family. I have tried to give you a glimpse of the world's cuisines that I have been fortunate to learn from and experience, highlighting their uniqueness and rejoicing in their commonalities.

Although the recipes are not the most authentic representations of these dishes, they are delightful interpretations that you can enjoy on a low-carb diet. I hope to be a bridge to the flavors of these traditional cuisines and spark in my readers some of the appreciation for them that I feel so deeply. You will find that I've also taken creative liberties with some dishes, often in the form of an Indian influence.

I hope this book makes you feel like you took a little trip around the world with me. More importantly, I hope it makes eating healthy fun, as it should be.

General Guidance

INGREDIENTS

Unless otherwise specified, in this book, eggs are large, olive oil is extra-virgin, salt is table salt, and butter is unsalted.

I often specify the type of oil to use for a particular recipe—for example, olive oil for sautéing, versus avocado oil for the higher temperatures of the air fryer or oven. You can use other oils if you prefer, but please be aware of the smoke point of the oil and use it appropriately.

I use a nonstick spray to grease my baking pans. I also often use an olive oil spray or avocado oil spray to toast bread.

Be sure to review the ingredient list before you begin each recipe, to make sure you don't miss any important timing information—for example, I may have called for cooked chickpeas, or beans soaked overnight.

Any Parmesan used is vegetarian; however, if you are not particular about using rennet-free cheeses, then go ahead and use your favorite variety.

Greek yogurt is not the same as Greek-style yogurt. For the best results and nutritional benefits, use Greek yogurt where specified in this book.

For the best results, use blanched almond flour as called for in various recipes in the book and not almond meal. Blanched almond flour has a finer and lighter texture than almond meal, as it is made from skinned almonds.

Specialty ingredients from various cuisines are used in several recipes in this book and can be purchased in specialty stores or online. I've also specified substitutions wherever possible.

EQUIPMENT

Invest in a scale and weigh all your ingredients for best results. I've provided all measurements in this book in both volume and metric units. (Note, where "cups" are specified, I am referring to US cups.) In this book, 1 tsp. = 5ml and 1 Tbsp. = 15ml.

The recipes in this book call for cooking in a (convection or fan) oven, an air-fryer, or a pressure cooker. Settings for these devices may vary, so use the visual indicators provided in each recipe as a guide and adjust your cooking times and temperatures as needed (I have an Instant Pot pressure cooker and have provided settings for it when used). If you have a conventional oven, you can increase the cooking time by about 20% as a general rule of thumb. When I call for small, medium, and large cooking pans in my recipes, I mean 8 in/20cm, 10 in/26cm and 12 in/30cm respectively.

NUTRITION

Nutritional information is provided on a best-efforts basis and intended as a general guide of nutritional content only. Please see the nutritional disclaimer in the appendix for more details.

Carbs and protein provide 4 calories of energy per gram, while fat provides 9 calories of energy per gram. In the Nutrition Per Serving donut chart for each recipe, the donut segments represent the total calories per serving provided by each macronutrient, while the label indicates the amount of each macronutrient in grams. (See the explanation for Zucchini Bread nutrition chart, opposite.)

In the nutritional information provided, the carb content includes fiber and the fiber content is specified separately, per convention in the United States. To calculate net carbs, deduct fiber from the carbs. For example, in the **Zucchini Bread** (page 14), net carbs per slice = 10g - 3g = 7g.

Most of the recipes in this book can be veganized using the suggestions provided. Please be aware that nutritional information, texture, and taste may change significantly when modifying a non-vegan recipe to be vegan.

Recipes in this book are predominantly gluten-free. But this is not specifically a gluten-free cookbook. If you have a gluten-free dietary requirement, then please exercise extra caution to ensure that your final product is suitable for your needs, and use gluten-free versions of ingredients such as tamari or soy sauce, gochujang sauce, oats, etc.

We are made of what we eat and what our food eats. To maximize nutritional value and help save our planet, choose pasture-raised or grass-fed dairy and eggs, and produce that is grown sustainably without the use of toxic chemicals.

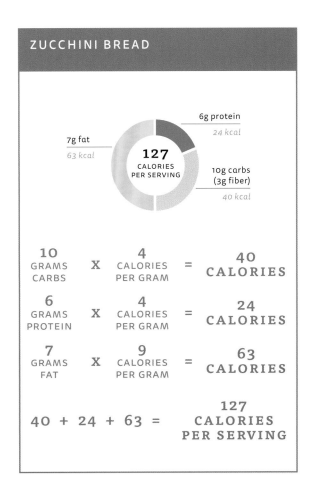

ZUCCHINI BREAD

6g protein
24 kcal

7g fat
63 kcal

127 CALORIES PER SERVING

10g carbs
(3g fiber)
40 kcal

10 GRAMS CARBS	X	4 CALORIES PER GRAM	=	40 CALORIES
6 GRAMS PROTEIN	X	4 CALORIES PER GRAM	=	24 CALORIES
7 GRAMS FAT	X	9 CALORIES PER GRAM	=	63 CALORIES

40 + 24 + 63 = 127 CALORIES PER SERVING

Zucchini Bread | 14

Chickpea Crepes | 18

Avocado Toast | 20

Pav Bhaji | 23

Roasted Red Pepper and Spinach Quesadillas | 25

Injera with Misir Wat, Gomen, and Atakilt | 26

Dosas with Chutney | 30

Socca Pizza | 32

Eggplant Chile Cheese Toast | 35

Khachapuri | 36

BREADS

All breads are not created equal. I'll save you a rant here about mass-produced, ultra-processed supermarket breads and instead tell you that the reason you'll want to try my breads is the flavor. Meet chickpea flour (or besan or gram flour)—the superhero of this section. It will quickly become a staple in your pantry. I combine it with blanched almond flour to create my **Zucchini Bread** (page 14), which is so easy and versatile you will wonder how you ever did without it. I use it all over this book, not just in this chapter. Later in this section, you will also see

chickpea flour used to make **Socca Pizza** (page 32), a traditional flatbread that's a staple in the French and Italian Riviera, and a thinned-down version of the same batter that makes wonderful crepes. But wait—as a self-respecting South Indian, how could I leave you without a recipe for crispy **Dosas with Chutney** (page 30)?

I hope this chapter is a revelation to you and shows you how easy it is to make healthy breads from scratch that can be used across so many cuisines. And I hope you take away some favorites for your own use.

1 medium zucchini/courgette (7 oz/200g)

½ tsp + 1 pinch salt, divided

1 cup/120g chickpea flour

1 scant cup/100g blanched almond flour

1 Tbsp baking powder

1 Tbsp ground flaxseed

2 eggs

TO VEGANIZE

Use these ingredient amounts:

1 medium zucchini (7 oz/200g)

½ tsp + 1 pinch salt, divided

1 heaping cup/140g chickpea flour

1 heaping cup/120g blanched almond flour

1½ Tbsp baking powder

2 Tbsp ground flaxseed

6 Tbsp aquafaba (soaking liquid from a can of chickpeas)

Follow the recipe as instructed, omitting the eggs and adding the aquafaba in Step 5. Bake for 45–55 minutes.

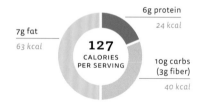

7g fat
63 kcal

6g protein
24 kcal

127 CALORIES PER SERVING

10g carbs (3g fiber)
40 kcal

Zucchini Bread

SERVES: 10

This low-carb, gluten-free, protein-rich bread has a mild savory flavor and gorgeous moist texture from the zucchini. It is endlessly versatile—use it for everything from grilled cheese to pav bhaji to breadcrumbs! It took me dozens of tries to perfect this recipe, but now it gets rave reviews, every time. I recommend you keep a loaf on standby in the freezer because it features in several recipes in this book, such as the **Avocado Toast** (page 20), **Pav Bhaji** (page 23), **Eggs Florentine** (page 137) and **French Onion Soup** (page 120).

This bread is dense and filling, so you will find that you cannot eat as much as you would of regular white or whole-wheat bread. Note that the vegan version will not rise as much as the original, but it tastes just as delicious and works better for **croutons** (page 109) and **breadcrumbs** (page 184).

Step 1. Grate the zucchini using the smaller holes of a box grater. Sprinkle a pinch of salt over the zucchini and let sit for 10–15 minutes to draw out moisture.

Step 2. Preheat the oven to 350°F/180°C. Lightly grease an 8½ x 4½ x 2½ in/20½ x 11 x 5½cm loaf pan.

Step 3. Combine the chickpea flour, almond flour, baking powder, flaxseed, and the remaining ½ teaspoon of salt in a large bowl and mix well. Beat the eggs lightly in a separate bowl.

Step 4. Place the zucchini in a thin towel, paper towel, or a nut-milk bag and squeeze over a bowl to get as much moisture out as possible (I usually get at least ¼ cup/60ml). Reserve the water for the next step.

Step 5. Add ¼ cup/60ml zucchini water, the beaten egg, and grated zucchini to the dry ingredients and stir well with a large spoon or whisk, breaking up any lumps. If the batter is too thick to combine, add a bit more zucchini water, 1 tablespoon at a time, up to 4 tablespoons, supplementing with regular water if needed. The batter should be thick, like a lump of wet sand.

Step 6. Transfer the batter to the prepared pan and tap gently on the counter to settle. Bake for 35–45 minutes, or until golden brown on top and a toothpick inserted in the center comes out clean.

Step 7. Let cool for 15–20 minutes. Loosen around the edges of the pan with a butter knife if necessary. Transfer to a flat surface to slice, and serve just as you would any other bread!

COOKING NOTES

Squeeze the zucchini hard to get as much moisture out as possible. This is the key to not ending up with a soggy mess!

Store the bread in an airtight container for 3–5 days at room temperature, or up to 3 months in the freezer. Defrost at room temperature for 4–5 hours or overnight.

Zucchini Bread,
page 14

Chickpea Crepes,
page 18

½ heaping cup/80g chickpea flour

½ tsp fine sea salt

½ tsp dried oregano

¾ cup + 2 Tbsp/210ml warm water

Chickpea Crepes

SERVES: 4

This is a tasty and versatile flatbread that can be used in many dishes, such as **Roasted Red Pepper and Spinach Quesadillas** (page 25), **Huevos Rancheros** (page 134), and as a stand in for **Injera** (page 26). This is the kind of recipe that takes practice, but I urge you to master it, as the possibilities are endless and exciting! Flavor your crepes with garlic or onion powder, add texture with chia seeds, nigella seeds, or sesame seeds, and use the finished crepes as a tortilla, roti, or wrap. See my **Mezze Platter** (page 142) for a fluffier version you can use in place of pita or garlic naan.

Step 1. Combine the chickpea flour, salt, and oregano in a bowl. Add ½ cup/120ml of warm water and whisk to combine until smooth, breaking up lumps. Add the remaining 6 Tbsp./90ml water and whisk until smooth. Let sit at room temperature for at least 2 hours, or up to 4 hours. The batter will be the consistency of heavy cream/ double cream.

Step 2. Lightly grease a small nonstick frying pan by rubbing a paper towel with a few drops of oil over it or using an oil spray. Heat over medium heat.

Step 3. When the pan is hot, stir the batter and pour ¼ cup/60ml of batter into the pan. The batter will sizzle as it hits the pan. Swirl the pan if necessary to coat the sides. Cook until you see the crepe dry completely on top and the edges get lightly browned, 2–3 minutes. Use a flat spatula to lift the edges up gently and peek at the bottom. If you cannot lift the edges up, that means the crepe is not done, so wait another minute.

Step 4. Flip the crepe carefully and cook the other side for 1 minute. Transfer to a plate to cool. Repeat to make 3 more crepes. Use as you would any flatbread or tortilla.

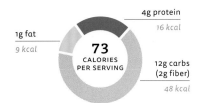

4g protein
16 kcal

1g fat
9 kcal

73
CALORIES
PER SERVING

12g carbs
(2g fiber)
48 kcal

It is important to rest the batter, so that the chickpea flour absorbs the water fully. You may find that the first crepe is a little hard to get off the pan—just let it cook longer until it is easy to flip. The pan will be at the right temperature and seasoned well for the second crepe.

Reduce the water to ¾ cup/180ml if you desire thicker crepes, for tacos, for example.

Wrap the crepes in foil and store in the fridge in a resealable bag for 2–3 days, or in the freezer for up to 3 months. Defrost at room temperature for 3–4 hours or overnight.

BALSAMIC TOMATOES

1 cup/150g diced cherry or grape tomatoes

1½ Tbsp balsamic vinegar

½ tsp fine sea salt

½ tsp cracked black pepper

AVOCADO SAUCE

1 medium avocado (7 oz/200g), scooped

¼ cup/40g roughly chopped onion

1 small jalapeño pepper

1 small bunch cilantro/fresh coriander (1 oz/25g)

2 cloves garlic

½ tsp salt

2 Tbsp lemon juice

4 slices **Zucchini Bread** (page 14), approximately 2 oz/55g each

---

TO VEGANIZE
Use vegan **Zucchini Bread** (page 14).

Avocado Toast

SERVES: 2

Do you need another avocado toast recipe in your life? I won't blame you if you're a bit fatigued by the average avocado toast, a ubiquitous item on every brunch menu. Still, I urge you to try this version. My flavorful zucchini bread comes alive when layered with a spicy avocado sauce and tangy balsamic tomatoes, making a triple-decker treat for your taste buds. Don't forget to chill the tomatoes—this really brings out the tang of the vinegar and brightens up this dish!

Step 1. Combine all the ingredients for the balsamic tomatoes and stir to mix. Refrigerate for at least 15 minutes.

Step 2. Combine all the ingredients for the avocado sauce in a food processor or blender and blend until smooth, adding 1–2 tablespoons water if needed.

Step 3. Lightly spray each slice of bread with oil and toast on both sides.

Step 4. Spread the avocado sauce evenly over each slice of toasted bread, then top with balsamic tomatoes. Serve immediately.

COOKING NOTES

For a less spicy sauce, seed the jalapeño before adding to the blender.

You may find that you don't need all the avocado sauce. Any leftovers can be used as pasta sauce (page 66), salad dressing, or a dip!

To store any extra avocado sauce, transfer to an airtight container, squeeze a lemon over the top, then refrigerate. This will help reduce oxidation, which can cause the top layer to turn brown. If it bothers you, simply skim off the top layer to reveal fresher-looking sauce below.

15g protein
60 kcal

29g fat
261 kcal

473
CALORIES
PER SERVING

38g carbs
(15g fiber)
152 kcal

BHAJI

1 Tbsp butter

1 cup/150g diced red onion

1 medium plum or Roma tomato
(4 oz/110g), diced

1 Tbsp tomato paste

2 tsp ground coriander seed

2 tsp paprika

1 tsp ground cumin

¼ tsp cayenne

2 cups/200g roughly chopped
cauliflower

¾ cup/120g frozen green peas

1 small red bell pepper/capsicum
(4 oz/110g), diced

¼ cup/30g yellow moong dal
(or split red lentils), soaked for
30 minutes and rinsed

1 tsp salt

⅔ cup/160ml water, plus more as
needed

1 Tbsp lemon juice

6 slices **Zucchini Bread**
(approximately 2 oz/55g each;
page 14)

2 tsp butter

2 Tbsp chopped cilantro/fresh
coriander, for garnish

4 lemon wedges, for garnish

> **TO VEGANIZE**
> Sub any neutral-flavored
> oil for the butter and use
> **Vegan Zucchini Bread**
> (page 14).

Pav Bhaji

SERVES: 3

Originally from the streets of Mumbai, pav bhaji is a crowd-pleaser that consists of a one-pot spicy vegetable mash (bhaji) served with soft dinner rolls (pav), garnished with a squeeze of lemon, chopped onions, cilantro, and often, dollops of butter! In my version, yellow moong dal works wonderfully as a substitute for starchy potato, lending the bhaji a nutty but creamy flavor. Served with toasted zucchini bread, this makes a hearty and delicious meal with no compromises! I often serve the bhaji over bread like a sloppy joe, so you get it all in one dreamy bite.

Step 1. Heat the butter in a large saucepan (for which you have a lid) over medium-high heat. Set aside 2 tablespoons of the diced onion for garnish and add the rest to the pan. Cook, stirring often, until the onions are lightly browned, about 5 minutes. Add the tomatoes, tomato paste, coriander, paprika, cumin, and cayenne. Mix well and cook until well incorporated and the tomatoes break down and start oozing, 3–4 minutes. Add a tablespoon of water to deglaze the pan if necessary.

Step 2. Add the cauliflower, peas, bell pepper, moong dal, salt, and water, and mix. Bring to a boil, reduce the heat to low, and simmer, covered, adding more water if needed, until the lentils are done, 20–30 minutes.

Step 3. Mash the vegetables and lentils together using a potato masher or pulse a few times with an immersion blender (the bhaji should still have some texture). Add the lemon juice and mix.

Step 4. Toast the bread in a skillet at medium heat using ½ teaspoon butter per slice. Serve the bread with bhaji. Garnish with cilantro and serve with the reserved chopped onion and lemon wedges.

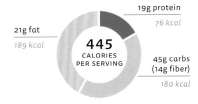

21g fat
189 kcal

19g protein
76 kcal

445 CALORIES PER SERVING

45g carbs
(14g fiber)
180 kcal

1 recipe **Chickpea Crepe** batter (page 18), prepared through step 1

FILLING

1 Tbsp olive oil

1 small red bell pepper/capsicum (4 oz/110g), cut into strips lengthwise

12 oz/340g fresh spinach (defrosted if frozen)

2 tsp minced garlic

¼ tsp salt

¼ tsp red chile flakes

½ cup/56g fresh mozzarella, torn into small pieces

SMOKED PAPRIKA YOGURT DIP

¼ cup/55g whole-milk plain Greek yogurt

1–2 Tbsp water, as needed

½ tsp smoked paprika

¼ tsp sea salt

> **TO VEGANIZE**
> Use vegan cheese or nutritional yeast in place of the mozzarella, and your preferred vegan yogurt for the dip.

Roasted Red Pepper and Spinach Quesadillas

SERVES: 2

An excellent way to use the **Chickpea Crepes** on page 18 is to make quesadillas. Feel free to change up the filling as you please!

Step 1. As the crepe batter rests, heat a frying pan over medium-high heat. When the pan is hot, add the olive oil and bell pepper and cook until the peppers are fork-tender, 2–3 minutes. You can also close the lid of the pan for a minute or two to let the peppers cook faster and brown in spots. Add the spinach gradually and cook, stirring, until it just wilts, about 5 minutes. Mix in the garlic, salt, and chile flakes and cook for another minute. Transfer to a plate.

Step 2. Return the same pan to medium heat. Stir the crepe batter and pour ¼ cup/60ml batter into the pan. The batter will sizzle as it hits the pan. Swirl the pan if necessary to coat the sides and cook until you see the crepe dry completely on top and the edges get lightly browned, 2–3 minutes. Use a spatula to lift the edges up gently and peek at the bottom. If you cannot lift the edges up, that means the crepe is not done, so wait another minute. Flip the crepes carefully and cook the other side for 1 minute.

Step 3. Flip the crepes back to the original side and spoon some of the spinach-pepper filling on one half. Sprinkle with cheese, fold the crepe, and cook on each side until the cheese melts, about 1 minute. Repeat with the remaining 3 crepes.

Step 4. Whisk together all the ingredients for the yogurt dip in a small bowl. Serve the filled crepes with the yogurt dip.

COOKING NOTES

It is important to rest the batter, so that the chickpea flour absorbs the water fully and is easier to work with.

You may find that the first crepe is a little hard to get off the pan—just let it cook longer until it is easy to flip. The pan will be at the right temperature and seasoned well for the second crepe.

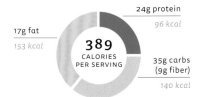

17g fat
153 kcal

24g protein
96 kcal

389 CALORIES PER SERVING

35g carbs (9g fiber)
140 kcal

MISIR WAT (LENTILS)

1 Tbsp niter kibbeh, ghee, or butter

2 medium onions (7 oz/200g), finely diced

2 ripe plum or Roma tomatoes (8 oz/225g), diced

1 Tbsp berbere

1 Tbsp minced garlic

1 tsp grated ginger

2 cups/480ml water, plus more as needed

¾ cup/90g split red lentils

¾ tsp salt

ATAKILT (MIXED VEGETABLES)

1 Tbsp niter kibbeh, ghee, or butter

1 medium onion (4 oz/110g), diced

2 small carrots (4 oz/110g), cut into ¾ inch/2-cm pieces

1 tsp grated ginger

1 tsp minced garlic

1 tsp ground cumin

1 tsp paprika

½ tsp ground turmeric

¼ tsp cayenne

½ head green cabbage (12 oz/340g), coarsely shredded

1 Tbsp water

½ tsp salt

(continued opposite)

9g fat
81 kcal

13g protein
52 kcal

293
CALORIES
PER SERVING

40g carbs
(9g fiber)
160 kcal

Injera with Misir Wat, Gomen, and Atakilt

SERVES: 6

In my early days of dining out in New York, I fell in love with family-style Ethiopian meals—an array of legume and vegetable preparations served on a fermented flatbread called injera. For anyone used to cooking Indian cuisine, these dishes also have an easy familiarity in the kitchen. In this recipe, we use my versatile **Chickpea Crepes** (page 18) as injera. I do perhaps go a little overboard and present three sides here as I find it hard to choose, but feel free to pick one or two if you are short on time. You can also make any of them ahead. Ethiopian food is usually cooked in niter kibbeh (spiced clarified butter), but you can also use ghee or butter if you can't find it. You can purchase berbere, a unique, spicy-sweet blend of spices, at a specialty store or online.

Step 1. For the misir wat, heat a medium saucepan (for which you have a lid) over medium-high heat. When the pan is hot, add the niter kibbeh and onions and cook, stirring, until the onions are lightly browned, about 5 minutes. Add the tomatoes, berbere, garlic, and ginger. Cook, stirring, and adding 1–2 tablespoons of water to deglaze the pan as needed, until the tomatoes break down and start oozing and the flavors are well melded, 4–5 minutes. Add the water, lentils, and salt and bring to a boil. Cover, reduce the heat to medium-low, and simmer until the lentils are completely cooked, 20–30 minutes. Set aside.

Step 2. For the atakilt, heat a medium sauté pan over medium heat. When the pan is hot, add the niter kibbeh, onions, and carrot and cook, stirring, until the carrots are half cooked and the onions are soft, about 5 minutes. Add the ginger, garlic, cumin, paprika, turmeric, and cayenne and cook for 1 minute. Add the cabbage, water, and salt. Mix well and cook, stirring often, until the carrots and cabbage are fully cooked, 15–20 minutes. Add more water to deglaze the pan if needed during cooking. Transfer to a bowl and use the same pan for the next step.

1 Tbsp niter kibbeh, ghee, or butter

1 medium onion (4 oz/110g), diced

2 tsp minced garlic

1 tsp grated ginger

1 tsp ground cumin

1 tsp ground coriander seed

½ tsp salt

12 oz/340g fresh spinach or other greens of choice, such as collard greens or kale, defrosted if frozen

INJERA (FLATBREAD)

2 batches **Chickpea Crepes** (page 18; 6–8 crepes)

TO VEGANIZE

Use olive oil in place of niter kibbeh, ghee, or butter.

Step 3. For the gomen, return the pan to medium heat. When the pan is hot, add the niter kibbeh and onions and cook, stirring, until onions the are soft, about 5 minutes. Add the garlic, ginger, cumin, coriander, and salt, mix well, and cook for 1 minute. Add the spinach and cook until just wilted.

Step 4. Prepare the chickpea crepes per the instructions (page 18). Serve the misir wat, atakilt, and gomen on the crepes, along with a side salad if desired.

*Injera with Misir Wat, Gomen,
and Atakilt, page 26*

Dosas with Chutney,
page 30

DOSAS

1 cup/120g yellow moong dal, soaked for 30 minutes and drained

1 in./2.5-cm piece ginger (or ¼ cup grated ginger)

1–2 Indian green chiles, jalapeño peppers, or Thai chiles

1 tsp salt

¾ cup/180ml water

4 tsp avocado oil, or other neutral oil of choice

PEANUT-GARLIC CHUTNEY

1 cup/112g dry-roasted unsalted peanuts

2 tsp store-bought tamarind concentrate paste, such as Tamicon, or 4 tsp fresh tamarind paste (page 184)

1–2 Indian green chiles, jalapeño peppers, or Thai chiles

1 medium clove garlic

½ tsp salt

⅓ cup/80ml water, plus more as needed

(continued opposite)

Dosas with Chutney

SERVES: 4

Growing up in South India, dosas with chutney were a regular breakfast or evening "tiffin" at home. My grandmother would make a large quantity of batter that we could use for a week or two at a stretch. Usually, the batter is made with rice and urad dal, soaked separately and ground, then fermented for several hours. This version is much simpler and does not require fermenting, but is still packed with flavor. Must you make both chutneys? Probably not, but life is so much better with variety!

Step 1. In a food processor, combine the dal, ginger, chiles, salt, and water and blend until smooth. Set aside.

Step 2. For each chutney, blend all the ingredients together in a small blender or food processor into a smooth paste. Add more water as needed, 1 tablespoon at a time, to blend. Set aside.

Step 3. To make the tadka, heat a small saucepan over medium-high heat. When hot, add the oil and mustard seeds. When the mustard seeds pop, add the urad dal and asafoetida and wait until the dal turns golden. Turn off the stove and divide the mixture over both chutneys.

Step 4. To cook the dosas, heat a large frying pan or griddle (nonstick works well) over medium-high heat for 3–4 minutes. When the pan is hot, ladle approximately one-fourth of the batter onto the center (you can also use a measuring cup if you don't have a ladle). Immediately spread the batter in a spiral motion from the center to the edges using the bottom of the ladle. Sprinkle 1 teaspoon of oil around the circumference and swirl the pan to help the oil coat the dosa surface underneath. The oil will sizzle as it hits the pan. When you see the top dry and the bottom get golden brown and crispy, flip the dosa and cook the other side for 1 minute. Transfer to a plate. Repeat for the 3 remaining dosas, turning the heat down slightly if needed. Serve hot with the chutneys.

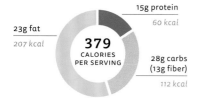

15g protein
60 kcal

23g fat
207 kcal

379
CALORIES
PER SERVING

28g carbs
(13g fiber)
112 kcal

1 large bunch cilantro/fresh
coriander (2 oz/55g)

3 Tbsp fresh or frozen shredded
coconut

1 Tbsp grated ginger

1 small Indian green chiles, jalapeño
peppers, or Thai chile

2 tsp store-bought tamarind
concentrate paste, such as Tamicon,
or 4 tsp fresh tamarind paste
(page 184)

¼ tsp salt

¼ cup/60ml water, plus more as
needed

TADKA (TEMPERING)

2 tsp avocado oil, or other neutral oil
of choice

1 tsp black mustard seeds

½ tsp urad dal (split and skinned
black gram)

¼ tsp asafoetida (hing, sometimes
called yellow powder)

COOKING NOTES

The process of spreading dosa batter (Step 4) may seem
intimidating. If the first one is a mess, don't worry, just scrape it
off and try again—the pan will likely be conditioned better. I also
recommend watching a quick video on YouTube to get familiar
with the process.

SOCCA BATTER

1 cup/120g chickpea flour

1 tsp dried oregano

½ tsp fine sea salt

1½ cups/360ml warm water

½ Tbsp olive oil

SMOKED EGGPLANT SAUCE

1 large eggplant/aubergine
(1 lb 3 oz/550g)

3–4 cloves garlic, sliced thinly
lengthwise

1 Indian green chile, or jalapeño or
Thai chile, chopped

1½ tsp olive oil, divided

½ cup/80g chopped onion

1 tsp ground cumin

¾ tsp fine sea salt

PIZZA

1 Tbsp olive oil

½ cup/56g fresh mozzarella, thinly
sliced

1 small jalapeño pepper, sliced and
seeded to adjust spice level to taste

2 Tbsp finely chopped fresh Italian
parsley

TO VEGANIZE

Use your favorite non-dairy
cheese or nutritional yeast,
or simply skip the cheese
and relish the eggplant
sauce on its own.

16g fat
144 kcal

360
CALORIES
PER SERVING

16g protein
64 kcal

38g carbs
(10g fiber)
152 kcal

Socca Pizza

SERVES: 3

While there are many things to love about the French Riviera, for me, the accessibility and variety of vegetarian foods was a delightful discovery. In Nice, we had socca, a simple chickpea-flour flatbread that is incredibly versatile. Here I pair it with a somewhat unusual pizza sauce made of smoked eggplant (à la babaghanoush or baingan bharta). Topped with fresh mozzarella slices and jalapeño, this is an easy dinner that promises to be a treat. Feel free to mix up the sauce and toppings to your liking.

Step 1. Mix the flour, oregano, and salt in a bowl. Whisk in the warm water gradually, smoothing out any lumps. Add the olive oil and mix well. Allow to sit for at least 30 minutes, or up to 4 hours.

Step 2. While the batter is resting, preheat an air fryer to 400°F/200°C or the oven to 450°F/230°C. Cut 6–8 slits in the eggplant with a knife, and stuff them with the garlic cloves and green chile. Brush the eggplant with ½ teaspoon of oil. Air fry for 20 minutes, turning halfway, or bake for 30–40 minutes, turning halfway. The eggplant should be charred and oozing out liquid, with the skin peeling off in spots. Let cool. Peel back the skin, scoop out the flesh, and mash it with a fork. Any liquid can be mixed into the mashed eggplant.

Step 3. Heat the remaining 1 teaspoon of oil in a medium sauté pan over medium-high heat. Add the onions and cook, stirring occasionally, until lightly caramelized, about 5 minutes. Turn the heat down to medium, add the mashed eggplant, cumin, and salt, and cook for 4–5 minutes more. Set aside.

Step 4. Preheat the broiler. Heat a large (12 in/30 cm) oven-safe skillet over medium-high heat and add the oil when the pan is hot. Stir the batter and pour it into the skillet. Cook for 6–8 minutes, until the bottom is golden brown and the top is dry. Turn off the stove. Spread the eggplant sauce over the crust, then top with the mozzarella and jalapeño. Broil for 2–3 minutes, or until the cheese melts and the sides get crispy. Garnish with the parsley, slice, and serve.

COOKING NOTES

If you don't have an oven-safe skillet, you can skip the broiling—just add a little extra oil to the pan in Step 4 to get the flatbread crispier, and cook the pizza for a few minutes after adding the toppings to melt the cheese. (If you have a lid for the skillet, cook the pizza with the lid closed).

BATTER

¼ cup/30g chickpea flour

3 Tbsp warm water

1 tsp avocado oil, or other neutral oil of choice

¼ tsp salt

¼ tsp dried oregano

½ large eggplant/aubergine (9 oz/250g), widest part sliced into 4 flat discs about ¾ inch/2cm thick

CHILE CHEESE TOPPING

¼ cup/28g grated Cheddar cheese

¼ cup/28g grated low-moisture mozzarella

2 Indian green chiles, jalapeño peppers, or Thai chiles, chopped and seeded to adjust spice level to taste

1 tsp grated ginger

1 tsp minced garlic

½ tsp ground cumin

¼ tsp salt

1 Tbsp chopped cilantro/fresh coriander, for garnish

TO VEGANIZE
Use vegan cheese and nutritional yeast for the topping, or skip the cheese.

Eggplant Chile Cheese Toast

SERVES: 2

Chile cheese toast is probably one of India's top five street food creations. Here we reimagine the recipe and sneak in vegetables by using eggplant slices as "toast" and topping them with the spiced cheese filling. Note that the eggplant "toast" will have some crunchiness where the batter crisps up, but will still be soft compared to actual toast. For a more traditional texture, you can make this recipe with my **Zucchini Bread** (page 14)—skip the batter at the left, and just toast the bread for a few minutes on the stove or in the oven.

Step 1. Whisk together all the ingredients for the batter and let sit for 1 hour at room temperature.

Step 2. Preheat the air fryer to 400°F/200°C or the oven to 450°F/235°C.

Step 3. Brush the eggplant slices with batter on both sides. Lay the eggplant flat on the base and airfry, until golden brown and dry on both sides, for 10 minutes, then flip using tongs and air fry 2 more minutes. (I can do two slices at a time in my air fryer, so I repeat this step for the remaining slices; yours may be larger). If using the oven, line a baking sheet with parchment paper and place the eggplant slices on it. Bake on one side for 13–15 minutes, or until golden brown, then flip and cook the other side for 3–5 minutes.

Step 4. As the eggplant cooks, mix all the ingredients for the chile cheese topping in a bowl.

Step 5. Sprinkle the cheese topping on the eggplant slices in the air fryer and air fry again for 1 ½ minutes, or bake for 2–3 minutes, until the cheese has completely melted. Garnish with cilantro and serve.

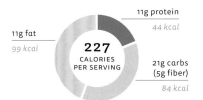

11g fat
99 kcal

11g protein
44 kcal

227 CALORIES PER SERVING

21g carbs (5g fiber)
84 kcal

DOUGH

½ cup/56g blanched almond flour

½ cup/60g chickpea flour

1 tsp baking powder

½ tsp fine sea salt

3 Tbsp warm whole milk

2 Tbsp olive oil

FILLING

¼ cup/28g fresh mozzarella,
torn into small pieces

¼ cup/55g whole-milk ricotta

¼ cup/28g crumbled feta

¼ cup/28g crumbled goat cheese

2 tsp cornstarch/cornflour, for
dusting

1 egg yolk, lightly beaten, for egg
wash

1 egg

2 tsp cold butter

2 tsp finely chopped fresh Italian
parsley or cilantro/fresh coriander,
for garnish

Pinch red chile flakes, for garnish

Khachapuri

SERVES: 4

CHEESE BOAT. Do I have your attention? This recipe is an adaptation of the Adjaruli khachapuri that I had at a Georgian restaurant called Oda House in NYC. Originally, I had tried it with store-bought pizza dough, but eventually ended up creating this low-carb dough that is easy to prepare and decidedly more delicious. (Sometimes I use it for flatbread pizza). Here we use a variety of cheeses that meld well together, in place of the special Georgian cheese called sulguni. I would serve this recipe as a family-style starter for four, but you could also use it as a main.

Step 1. Combine the almond flour, chickpea flour, baking powder, and sea salt in a bowl. Add the milk and oil and mix with a spoon to make a soft, lightly sticky dough, the texture of clay. Knead a little with your hands and form a ball. Cover with plastic wrap and refrigerate for at least 30 minutes or up to 4 hours.

Step 2. Preheat the oven to 350°F/180°C.

Step 3. For the filling, combine all 4 cheeses in a bowl and mix well. Set aside.

Step 4. Dust a piece of parchment paper the size of a baking sheet with the cornstarch. Place the dough on the parchment. Using a rolling pin, roll the dough into a chubby oval shape, about 10 in/25cm long and 1/16 in/2mm thick. Spoon the cheese filling into the center and flatten it slightly with the back of the spoon. Using your fingers, roll up the sides, folding over the dough to make a wall. Pinch and twist the ends to form a boat shape, as shown in the picture. The dough is quite forgiving, so redistribute dough as needed and flatten the cheese to fill the boat.

Step 5. Transfer the parchment with the dough to the baking sheet, brush the top and sides of the dough boat with egg yolk, and bake for 15 minutes. Remove the baking sheet from the oven and leave the oven on. Using a spoon, make a well in the center of the cheese filling and carefully crack the egg into it. Add a teaspoon of butter on each side of the egg and bake for an additional 10–12 minutes, or until the egg white is set but the yolk jiggles. Garnish with cilantro and chile flakes and serve immediately.

13g protein
52 kcal

24g fat
216 kcal

328
CALORIES
PER SERVING

15g carbs
(3g fiber)
60 kcal

RICE

Rice is comfort, be it a fragrant pulao in India, a paella in Spain, or a risotto in Italy. I grew up in South India where rice is a staple food, and my body still craves it with every meal. In fact, lack of portion control with rice has often been my healthy-eating downfall.

In this section, I use riced cauliflower to re-create some of my favorite rice dishes from across the world. Why cauliflower rice, and not other whole grains such as quinoa or even brown rice? For me, cauliflower rice is the closest substitute for white rice. When cooked properly, it comes closest to mimicking the texture of the real thing, and it's mild and absorbs flavors well. Quinoa and brown rice, while great options, have a distinctive taste and texture and tend to stand out; whereas cauliflower rice is a wonderful carrier for other ingredients in the dish and lets them shine. It is also inexpensive, widely available, extremely easy to make, and gluten-free, plus it gives you an extra serving of vegetables with your meal.

If prepared cauliflower rice is available, either fresh or frozen works well in these recipes (I tend to buy the frozen version, as it is more convenient to store, and defrost it directly on the stovetop). To make your own, just grate cauliflower using the larger holes of a box grater or chop into large florets and blitz in a food processor.

Feel free to substitute the cauliflower rice in these recipes with the whole grains of your choice, but remember that your methods of preparation may have to change. For example, you will need more water to cook grains like brown rice or quinoa.

KADHI

3 cups/720ml water

1 cup/220g whole-milk plain Greek yogurt or non-dairy yogurt

1 Tbsp chickpea flour (see cooking note)

2 tsp avocado oil or other neutral oil of choice

1 tsp mustard seeds

1 tsp cumin seeds

¼ tsp fenugreek seeds (optional)

8–10 fresh curry leaves (double the quantity if using dried)

1 dry red Indian chile (optional)

1 Tbsp grated ginger

1 Tbsp minced garlic

1 tsp salt

½ tsp ground turmeric

¼ tsp cayenne

JEERA RICE

1 Tbsp ghee, butter, or vegetable oil

1 tsp cumin seeds

1 cinnamon stick

1 bay leaf

2 whole cloves

¼ cup/40g finely chopped onion

1 lb/450g cauliflower rice

½ tsp salt

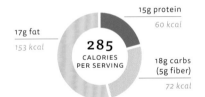

17g fat
153 kcal

15g protein
60 kcal

285
CALORIES
PER SERVING

18g carbs
(5g fiber)
72 kcal

Kadhi with Jeera Rice

SERVES: 2

When I started on my low-carb culinary journey, I began to look at some traditional Indian dishes with new eyes. Naturally protein-rich, kadhi is a yogurt-based curry that is thickened with chickpea flour, tempered with spices, and slow-cooked. The Punjabi version is spicier and usually served with pakoras while the Gujarati version is milder, with a hint of sweetness; mine is closer to the former. It is served here with a cauliflower jeera "rice" that will quickly become your go-to for every curry.

Step 1. In a large bowl, whisk together the water, yogurt, and chickpea flour until smooth.

Step 2. Heat the oil in a large saucepan over medium heat. When the oil is hot, add the mustard seeds and wait until they crackle, then add the cumin seeds and fenugreek seeds, if using. When the cumin seeds turn dark brown, add the curry leaves, dry red chile, if using, ginger, and garlic and sauté for 30 seconds. Add the salt, turmeric, and cayenne and mix well.

Step 3. Add the chickpea flour–yogurt mixture to the pan and stir well. Bring to a boil, then reduce the heat to medium-low and simmer until thick (like heavy cream or double cream), 20–25 minutes.

Step 4. To make the jeera rice, heat the ghee in a medium (10 inch/26-cm) sauté pan over medium heat. Add the cumin seeds, cinnamon stick, bay leaf, and cloves and cook, stirring, until fragrant, 2–3 minutes. Add the onion, increase the heat to medium-high, and cook, stirring often, until lightly brown, about 5 minutes. Add the cauliflower rice and salt, mix well, and reduce the heat to medium. Cook, stirring, until dry and heated throughout, 10–15 minutes.

COOKING NOTES

If you feel the kadhi is not thickening fast enough, you can whisk in another tablespoon of chickpea flour.

You can freeze leftover kadhi for up to 2 months in an airtight container. Once defrosted, you might need to pulse the gravy a couple of times with an immersion blender to fix the consistency.

1½ cups/180g dried dark red kidney beans, soaked overnight and rinsed, or 3 (15-oz/400-g) cans kidney beans, drained and rinsed

1½ cups/360ml water

2 Tbsp avocado oil, or neutral oil

1 tsp cumin seeds

1 medium onion (7 oz/200g), diced

1 bay leaf

1 Tbsp grated ginger

1 Tbsp minced garlic

1 Indian green chile, or jalapeño pepper, or Thai chile, chopped

3 medium plum or Roma tomatoes (11 oz/300g), diced

1 tsp paprika

1 tsp garam masala

¾ tsp ground coriander seed

¼ tsp ground turmeric

1 tsp salt

JEERA RICE

1 Tbsp ghee, butter, or oil

1 tsp cumin seeds

1 cinnamon stick

1 bay leaf

2 whole cloves

2 Tbsp finely chopped onion

1 lb/450g cauliflower rice

½ tsp salt

2 Tbsp finely chopped cilantro/fresh coriander, for garnish

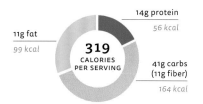

11g fat
99 kcal

319
CALORIES
PER SERVING

14g protein
56 kcal

41g carbs
(11g fiber)
164 kcal

Rajma Chawal

SERVES: 4

In a South Indian household, it is often a treat to eat North Indian food (and the reverse is usually true in North Indian homes!). We would excitedly await the day that my mom would make rajma, a hearty Punjabi dish that resembles a chili, with dark red kidney beans cooked in a delicious onion-tomato gravy. When served with this delectable cauliflower jeera "rice" (chawal), it is indeed a treat.

Step 1. Combine the beans and water in a pressure cooker and cook until soft (30 minutes on high pressure, natural release in an Instant Pot). Reserve the water. Skip this step if using canned beans.

Step 2. As the beans cook, heat a medium saucepan over medium-high heat to make the sauce. Add the oil and cumin seeds, and when they turn brown, add the onions and bay leaf. Cook, stirring occasionally, for about 10 minutes, until the onions are deep golden brown. Add the ginger, garlic, and chile and cook for 1 minute. Add the tomatoes, paprika, garam masala, coriander, and turmeric and cook for about 5 minutes, stirring often, until fully incorporated and the tomatoes break down and start oozing. Deglaze the pan with 1 tablespoon of water if necessary. Remove the bay leaf and let cool.

Step 3. Add 2 tablespoons of cooked beans to the saucepan and blend with an immersion blender until smooth.

Step 4. Add the remaining beans along with the bean water (or ¾ cup/180ml plain water, or more as needed, if using canned beans) to the saucepan. Add the salt and mix well. Bring to a boil and simmer, uncovered, stirring occasionally, for 10–15 minutes, until the flavors are fully melded and the gravy turns a deep reddish-brown.

Step 5. To make the jeera rice, heat the ghee in a medium (10 inch/26-cm) sauté pan over medium heat. Add the cumin seeds, cinnamon stick, bay leaf, and cloves and cook, stirring, for 2–3 minutes, or until fragrant. Add the onion, increase the heat to medium-high, and cook, stirring often, until lightly brown, about 5 minutes. Add the cauliflower rice and salt, mix well, and reduce the heat to medium. Sauté until dry and heated throughout, 10–15 minutes.

Step 6. Garnish the rajma with cilantro and serve with the jeera rice.

MUJADDARA

1 Tbsp + 1 tsp olive oil, divided

1¼ cups/200g thinly sliced onion

12 oz/340g cauliflower rice

1½ cups/360ml water

⅓ cup/60g green or brown lentils

1 large clove garlic, minced

2 tsp roasted ground cumin (see Cooking Notes)

1 bay leaf

1 tsp fine sea salt

½ tsp cracked black pepper

1 Tbsp finely chopped fresh Italian parsley

TZATZIKI

1 medium cucumber (7 oz/200g), grated

½ tsp fine sea salt, plus more for salting cucumber

1 cup/220g whole-milk plain Greek yogurt

1 large clove garlic, minced

1 Tbsp finely chopped fresh dill or mint

1 Tbsp lemon juice

1 tsp olive oil

¼ tsp cracked black pepper

TO VEGANIZE

Make the tzatziki with your preferred vegan yogurt in place of the whole-milk yogurt.

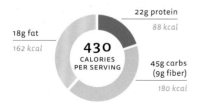

18g fat
162 kcal

22g protein
88 kcal

430
CALORIES
PER SERVING

45g carbs
(9g fiber)
180 kcal

Mujaddara with Tzatziki

SERVES: 2

Almost every region has its version of seasoned rice and beans, and the Middle East is no exception. For me, the highlight of mujaddara is the deeply caramelized onions that are simply irresistible. The dish also uses lentils, which largely retain their shape and give the dish its name: "mujaddara" means "pockmarked" or "pimpled" in Arabic. In this version, we cook the cauliflower rice and lentils separately to maximize texture.

Tzatziki, meanwhile, is a similar preparation to the Indian raita, but is usually thicker and creamier in consistency because it is made with Greek yogurt. I find the pairing of these dishes particularly alluring as a complete meal. For a full Middle Eastern spread, serve with a **Mezze Platter** (page 142) and **Falafel Salad** (page 87).

Step 1. In a medium sauté pan, heat 1 tablespoon of olive oil over medium-high heat. Add the onions and cook, stirring often, until deep golden brown and caramelized, 7–10 minutes. Set aside.

Step 2. In the same pan, heat the remaining 1 teaspoon of oil over medium heat. Add the cauliflower rice and sauté until dry, 10–15 minutes.

Step 3. As the cauliflower rice cooks, bring the water to a boil in a medium saucepan. Add the lentils, garlic, cumin, bay leaf, salt, and pepper. Cover and simmer, until the lentils are cooked and the water has evaporated, 15–20 minutes.

Step 4. Meanwhile, make the tzatziki. Sprinkle the cucumber lightly with salt and let sit for 5 minutes. Squeeze out the moisture using a thin towel. Mix the cucumber and all the remaining ingredients together in a bowl and refrigerate until ready to serve.

Step 5. Add the cooked lentil mixture to the cauliflower rice in the pan, along with half the caramelized onions and half the parsley. Garnish the mujaddara with the remaining caramelized onions and parsley and serve with tzatziki.

COOKING NOTES

You can use regular ground cumin for this recipe, but believe me when I say that roasted cumin is a game-changer! Dry-roast cumin seeds on medium-low heat for a few minutes, then blitz in a spice grinder. Don't have a spice grinder? A tester gave me a simple shortcut—just dry roast your ground cumin itself before using!

1 Tbsp + 1 tsp olive oil, divided

1 lb/450g cauliflower rice

1 small onion (4 oz/110g), diced

1 small red bell pepper/capsicum (4 oz/110g), sliced lengthwise into thin strips

1 Tbsp minced garlic

20 green beans (4 oz/110g), ends trimmed and sliced in half

1 (14 ½-oz/400-g) can chickpeas, drained

2 tsp paprika

1 tsp smoked paprika

1 tsp fine sea salt

½ tsp cracked black pepper

Pinch of saffron

1 cup/260g canned diced tomatoes (two-thirds of a 14 ½-oz/400-g can)

1 cup/240 ml vegetable broth or water

2 marinated artichoke hearts, quartered

½ cup/80g frozen green peas

6–8 large green or black olives, sliced

2–3 sprigs rosemary

1 Tbsp chopped fresh Italian parsley, for garnish

4 lemon wedges, for garnish

Vegetable Paella

SERVES: 4

I started on my paella journey after watching a chef make it with great flair by the beach. Usually made with a short-grain rice such as Spanish bomba, this paella is made with cauliflower rice, which absorbs the flavors surprisingly well. It is loosely based on the Valenciana style, fragrant with saffron and rosemary. Whether indoors or outdoors, this is a great summer party dish that's easy to make and easy on the eyes. Add my **Gazpacho Smoothies** (page 166) and **Patatas Bravas** (page 159) to make it a feast.

Step 1. In a medium sauté pan, heat 1 teaspoon of olive oil over medium heat. Add the cauliflower rice and sauté until dry, 10–15 minutes. Transfer to a bowl and set aside.

Step 2. Add the remaining 1 tablespoon of olive oil to the same pan, add the onions, bell pepper, and garlic, and sauté over medium heat for 3–4 minutes. Add the green beans, chickpeas, paprika, smoked paprika, salt, pepper, and saffron, reduce the heat to medium-low, and sauté for 3–4 minutes. Add the tomatoes and cook for about 5 more minutes.

Step 3. Add the broth or water and bring to a boil. Add the cauliflower rice and stir to distribute evenly. Simmer, uncovered, without stirring, until the water has mostly evaporated, 10–15 minutes.

Step 4. Scatter the artichokes, peas, olives, and rosemary on top, gently pressing down to incorporate. Do not stir. Cook, uncovered, for a few more minutes until dry and you no longer see water bubbling to the surface a few more minutes, (you can press down gently with a spatula to help any water bubble up).

Step 5. Optionally, turn up the heat to high for 1–2 minutes to char the bottom of the rice. This creates a crispy crust, called the soccarat, at the bottom. Remove the rosemary, garnish with parsley and lemon wedges, and serve.

10g protein
40 kcal

8g fat
72 kcal

244
CALORIES
PER SERVING

33g carbs
(10g fiber)
132 kcal

6 tsp toasted sesame oil, divided

½ lb/225g cauliflower rice

1 small cucumber or 2 baby cucumbers (6 oz/160g)

Pinch of gochugaru (Korean chile flakes) or regular chile flakes

1–2 tsp fine sea salt

1 cup/100g mung bean sprouts

4 tsp minced garlic, divided

2 Tbsp white sesame seeds, divided

2 cups/60g spinach (defrosted if frozen)

⅔ cup/100g sliced red bell pepper/ capsicum, cut into matchsticks

½ cup/50g sliced white mushrooms

2 tsp gochujang sauce or Sriracha

2 eggs

> **TO VEGANIZE**
> Use **Seared Tofu** (page 70) or **Tempeh** (page 99) as the protein instead of the egg.

Vegetable Bibimbap

SERVES: 2

Hangawi is a wonderful (and rare) *vegetarian* Korean establishment in NYC that serves vegetable bibimbap in a classic stone bowl that arrives sizzling to your table. It has seasoned vegetables atop white rice, along with a spicy sauce called gochujang, stirred together before eating. In my version, the rice takes a back seat, because I wanted to highlight the simple yet flavorful preparation of vegetables and the versatility of the toppings. This dish lends itself well to meal prep, as the vegetables can be prepared ahead of time. Feel free to use the toppings of your choice—for example, you can add kimchi or other pickled vegetables, zucchini, carrots, and so on.

Step 1. Heat 1 teaspoon of oil in a medium sauté pan over medium heat. Add the cauliflower rice and sauté until dry, 10–15 minutes. Transfer to a bowl and set the pan aside to use in Step 3.

Step 2. Slice the cucumbers as desired (I use a mandoline slicer with a crinkle-cut attachment). Sprinkle with gochugaru flakes and a pinch of salt, toss, and refrigerate.

Step 3. Heat 1 teaspoon of oil in the pan over medium heat. Add the bean sprouts, ½ teaspoon of garlic, 1 teaspoon of sesame seeds, and sprinkle with salt to taste. Cook until just tender, 4–5 minutes, transfer to a bowl, and set aside. Repeat with the spinach, bell pepper, and mushrooms, cooking each topping individually until tender and adding another teaspoon of oil, ½ teaspoon of garlic, 1 teaspoon of sesame seeds, and a sprinkle of salt to each one. Transfer to separate bowls.

Step 4. Combine the remaining oil, 1 teaspoon of sesame seeds, and 1½ teaspoons of garlic with the gochujang sauce.

Step 5. In a lightly greased nonstick frying pan, over medium heat, fry the eggs sunny-side up.

Step 6. Divide the cauliflower rice between two bowls. Surround the rice with cucumbers, bean sprouts, spinach, bell peppers, and mushrooms. Top each portion with a fried egg and gochujang and serve.

COOKING NOTES

You can prep the veggies a day in advance and store refrigerated. Fry the eggs just prior to serving.

14g protein
56 kcal

24g fat
216 kcal

348
CALORIES
PER SERVING

19g carbs
(7g fiber)
76 kcal

3 tsp olive oil, divided

1 lb/450g cauliflower rice

1 cup/100g small broccoli florets

½ cup/75g diced bell pepper/
capsicum

½ cup/80g frozen green peas

½ tsp dried oregano

1 tsp minced garlic

1 cup/240ml low-sodium vegetable
broth or water

¼ cup/28g grated Parmesan

1 Tbsp lemon zest (from 1 medium
lemon)

½ tsp cracked black pepper

¼ tsp red chile flakes

Salt (optional)

2 Tbsp heavy cream/double cream,
goat cheese, or cream cheese

1 Tbsp lemon juice

TO VEGANIZE
Use nutritional yeast in
place of the Parmesan (you
will likely need additional
salt), and vegan cream
cheese in place of the heavy
cream.

Lemon Risotto

SERVES: 2

This creamy and luxurious cauliflower rice risotto with a burst
of lemon is ready in under 30 minutes. It's just the thing for a
weeknight meal that cleans out the veggies in your fridge, but still
serves up an elegant dinner.

Step 1. Heat 1 teaspoon of olive oil in a medium sauté pan over
medium heat. Add the cauliflower rice and sauté until dry,
10–15 minutes. Set the rice aside.

Step 2. Heat the same pan over medium-high heat. When the
pan is hot, add the remaining 2 teaspoons of olive oil, the broccoli,
peppers, peas, and oregano. Sauté until fork-tender, 2–3 minutes.
Add the garlic and cook until fragrant, about 1 minute.

Step 3. Lower the heat to medium, add the cauliflower rice, broth,
Parmesan, lemon zest, pepper, and chile flakes, and simmer,
uncovered, until reduced and thick and the water has mostly
evaporated, 5–8 minutes. Taste and add salt if needed (the cheese is
quite salty).

Step 4. Stir in the heavy cream and lemon juice and serve.

17g fat
153 kcal

309
CALORIES
PER SERVING

13g protein
52 kcal

26g carbs
(8g fiber)
104 kcal

4 tsp toasted sesame oil or peanut oil, divided

1 lb/450g cauliflower rice

1 Tbsp rice vinegar or white vinegar

1¼ tsp salt

⅓ tsp cracked black pepper

1 cup/200g small broccoli florets

⅔ cup/100g shelled edamame (fresh or frozen), riced in a food processor if desired

2½ Tbsp grated ginger

1½ Tbsp minced or finely chopped garlic

4 medium scallions, chopped and divided into white and green parts

¼ tsp red chile flakes

Your favorite hot sauce (optional)

Ginger Fried Rice

SERVES: 2

This fried "rice" packs a ton of flavor despite not using soy sauce! As a bonus, you can make it entirely with frozen vegetables. I adapted chef Jean-Georges Vongerichten's technique from the *New York Times* for this recipe, where each ingredient is separately cooked to perfection and then layered. I have since learned that it is absolutely the best way to make any stir-fry.

Step 1. Heat a large (12 inch/30-cm) sauté pan or wok over medium heat and add 1 teaspoon of oil. Add the cauliflower rice and sauté until dry, 10–15 minutes. Add the vinegar, salt, and pepper and mix. Cook until the rice is dry and crisp, 2 minutes. Remove from the stove.

Step 2. Bring a pot of salted water to a boil and add the broccoli. When it turns bright green, add the edamame and cook for 1 minute. Drain, rinse in cold water, and pat dry. Set aside.

Step 3. In a separate small saucepan over medium heat, fry the ginger, garlic, white part of the scallions, and chile flakes in the remaining 3 teaspoons of oil until brown and crisp. Set aside.

Step 4. Heat the pan or wok with the cauliflower rice over medium heat, add the broccoli, edamame, and fried ginger-garlic mixture, and toss to combine. Season to your liking with salt and pepper and cook until heated throughout. Garnish with the green part of the scallions, drizzle with hot sauce, if using, and serve.

COOKING NOTES

I prefer this vegan, but you can also add a fried egg on top to ramp up the protein.

To make this a one-pot dish (you may sacrifice some texture), start with Step 3, frying the ginger-garlic mixture in the wok, and set it aside in a bowl. Then cook the cauliflower rice, broccoli, and edamame with 1 teaspoon of oil in the same pan until dry and the broccoli is fork-tender. Season with salt, pepper, and vinegar, add the ginger-garlic mixture, and toss.

14g protein
56 kcal

12g fat
108 kcal

264
CALORIES
PER SERVING

25g carbs
(11g fiber)
100 kcal

TAGINE

1 Tbsp olive oil

1 small onion (4 oz/110g), diced

1 small red or yellow bell pepper/
capsicum (4 oz/110g), diced

1 medium zucchini/courgette
(7 oz/200g), diced

1 Tbsp grated ginger

1 Tbsp minced garlic

1 tsp ground cumin

1 tsp ground coriander seed

1 tsp ground turmeric

1 tsp cracked black pepper

½ tsp cayenne

1 (15-oz/400-g) can diced tomatoes

1 (15-oz/400-g) can chickpeas or
heaping ½ cup/100g dried chickpeas,
soaked overnight and cooked

½ medium preserved lemon, diced,
or 1 Tbsp lemon zest + 1 pinch salt

1½ cups/360ml low-sodium
vegetable broth

½ tsp salt

8 oz/225g fresh spinach (defrosted if
frozen)

1 Tbsp lemon juice

LEMON-HERB RICE

1 tsp olive oil

1 lb/450g cauliflower rice

2 Tbsp chopped fresh Italian parsley

1 Tbsp lemon zest (from 1 medium
lemon)

1 Tbsp lemon juice

¾ tsp fine sea salt, plus more to taste

10g fat
90 kcal

302
CALORIES
PER SERVING

12g protein
48 kcal

41g carbs
(12g fiber)
164 kcal

Tagine with Lemon-Herb Rice

SERVES: 3

Chilly nights call out for this lemony tagine, brimming with chickpeas, spinach, and the goodness of warming spices. Of North African origin, the word "tagine" refers to both the dish that it is traditionally made in, as well as the stew itself. This recipe is more of an "instant" version but still has great flavor. I serve it here with a lemon-herb cauliflower rice in lieu of the traditional couscous.

Step 1. Heat a medium saucepan over medium heat. Add the olive oil and onions and cook, stirring, until the onions are soft, about 5 minutes. Add the bell pepper and zucchini and cook, stirring, until fork-tender, 3–4 minutes.

Step 2. Add the ginger, garlic, cumin, coriander, turmeric, pepper, and cayenne, mix well, and cook until fragrant, 1 minute.

Step 3. Add the tomatoes, chickpeas, preserved lemon, broth, and salt. Bring to a boil, reduce the heat, cover, and simmer until the flavors are well melded, 10–15 minutes.

Step 4. As the broth simmers, make the lemon-herb rice. Heat a medium sauté pan over medium heat. When hot, add the olive oil and cauliflower rice and cook, stirring, until dry, 10–15 minutes. Turn off the stove, add the parsley, lemon zest, lemon juice, and salt, and mix well.

Step 5. Uncover the tagine, add the spinach, and cook for 1 minute. Turn off the stove and let it finish cooking in the residual heat. Stir in the lemon juice. Serve the tagine and lemon-herb rice together.

COOKING NOTES

When Meyer lemons are in season, try making your own preserved lemon for this recipe—I like the tutorial from the website rainbowplantlife.com.

PICO DE GALLO

1 medium plum or Roma tomato (4 oz/110g), finely chopped

2 Tbsp finely chopped onion

2 Tbsp finely chopped cilantro/fresh coriander

1 Tbsp lemon juice

½ tsp fine sea salt

SPICED BLACK BEANS

1 (15-oz/400-g) can black beans, rinsed and drained (see cooking notes)

2 tsp olive oil

1 tsp minced garlic

1 tsp smoked paprika

½ tsp dried oregano

1 bay leaf

½ tsp salt

FAJITA VEGGIES

2 tsp olive oil

⅔ cup/100g thinly sliced onion

⅔ cup/100g thinly sliced green bell pepper/capsicum

½ tsp dried oregano

¼ tsp salt

CILANTRO-LIME RICE

1 tsp olive oil

1 lb/450g cauliflower rice

2 Tbsp lime juice

2 Tbsp chopped cilantro/fresh coriander

½ tsp salt

1 medium avocado (7 oz/200g), diced

½ cup/56g grated Cheddar cheese

TO VEGANIZE
Use vegan cheese or nutritional yeast instead of the Cheddar cheese.

Burrito Jars

SERVES: 4

This is a fresh and flavorful Chipotle Mexican Grill–inspired bowl that is wonderfully easy to make at home. Yes, there are a few distinct pieces of the puzzle, but I promise you they come together really quickly. Layer it in a mason jar to be the envy of your coworkers, or just serve it in a bowl for a fun make-your-own-burrito-bowl dinner!

Step 1. Mix all the ingredients for the pico de gallo in a bowl and refrigerate.

Step 2. Heat a medium sauté pan over medium heat. When hot, add all the ingredients for the black beans and mix. Cook, stirring, until the flavors are well melded, adding 1 tablespoon of water to deglaze the pan if needed, about 5 minutes. Divide equally among four jars or bowls.

Step 3. Heat the same pan over medium-high heat. When hot, add all the ingredients for the fajita veggies and mix. Cook, stirring occasionally, until the onions are lightly browned and the bell peppers are bright green and crisp, 3–4 minutes. Layer on top of the beans in the jars.

Step 4. For the Cilantro-Lime Rice, heat the oil in the same pan over medium heat. Add the cauliflower rice, and sauté until dry, 10–15 minutes. Turn off the stove, add the lime juice, cilantro, and salt, and mix well. Layer on top of the fajita veggies in the jars.

Step 5. Remove the pico de gallo from the fridge and layer on top of the rice. Top each jar with avocado and cheese and serve.

COOKING NOTES

If making your own black beans, use a heaping ½ cup/100g dried beans.

I used 12 oz/360ml mason jars for this recipe. Store the pico de gallo, avocado, and cheese separately if you would like to heat this up at work.

18g fat
162 kcal

13g protein
52 kcal

342
CALORIES
PER SERVING

32g carbs
(14g fiber)
128 kcal

1 cup/240ml water

½ cup/60g yellow moong dal, soaked for 30 minutes, drained, and rinsed

1 lb/450g cauliflower rice

1 tsp ghee, or butter

TOMATO CHUTNEY

1 Tbsp avocado oil, or other neutral oil of choice

½ tsp black mustard seeds

2–3 medium plum or Roma tomatoes (10 oz/280g)

1 tsp store-bought tamarind concentrate paste, such as Tamicon, or 2 tsp fresh tamarind paste (page 184)

½ tsp salt

¼ tsp cayenne

¼ tsp asafoetida (hing, sometimes called yellow powder)

TADKA (TEMPERING)

2 Tbsp ghee, or butter

1 tsp cumin seeds

2 Tbsp raw cashews, chopped

10–15 fresh curry leaves, chopped

2 tsp grated ginger

¾ tsp salt

¾ tsp cracked black pepper (if you have whole pepper, use a mix of whole pepper and cracked pepper)

TO VEGANIZE
Use any neutral oil in place of the ghee.

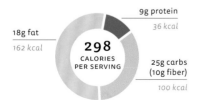

18g fat
162 kcal

9g protein
36 kcal

298
CALORIES
PER SERVING

25g carbs
(10g fiber)
100 kcal

Ven Pongal with Tomato Chutney

SERVES: 3

I take my comfort food very seriously, particularly when it comes to this dish, and have been delighted with the cauliflower rice version. Ven (white) Pongal is a homely mixture of rice and moong dal (like khichadi) that gets elevated to extraordinary by a spectacular tadka of spices in ghee. It is normally prepared for the harvest festival of South India (also called Pongal) along with a sweet version made of jaggery. I pair it here with my mother in-law's tomato chutney, which is to die for—you will want to make a big jar of it and slather it over everything.

Step 1. Bring the water to a boil in a medium saucepan. Add the dal, and simmer for about 20 minutes, or until cooked, adding more water as necessary. You can also pressure cook the dal (15 minutes on high pressure in an Instant Pot, natural release).

Step 2. Meanwhile, heat a medium sauté pan over medium heat. When hot, add the ghee and cauliflower rice and sauté until dry, 10–15 minutes. Transfer to a plate and set the pan aside to use in Step 4.

Step 3. To make the tomato chutney, heat a small saucepan over medium-high heat. When hot, add the oil and mustard seeds. When the mustard seeds pop, add all the remaining chutney ingredients and mix well. Cover, reduce the heat to low, and cook for 20–30 minutes, stirring often. The chutney is done when the tomatoes have disintegrated and the oil is oozing, turning into a thick paste with some texture from the tomato skins.

Step 4. To make the tadka, return the sauté pan to medium heat. When hot, add the ghee and cumin seeds. When the cumin seeds turn dark brown, add the cashews. When the cashews turn golden brown, add all the remaining tadka ingredients and cook, stirring, for 1–2 minutes, until fragrant.

Step 5. Add the cooked moong dal and cauliflower rice to the pan with the tadka and mix well using a spatula, until the dal and rice meld together and the tadka is distributed throughout. Taste, add more salt if needed, and serve.

PASTA AND NOODLES

Along with white rice, a bowl of pasta can make me go weak in the knees. So it was particularly surprising to me how easy it was to switch to vegetable alternatives. My goal here is to let the flavorful sauces shine and the noodles be humble carriers, while you still get the satisfaction of twirling them with your fork. Zucchini noodles are probably the most well-known pasta substitute, but there are quite a few options in the market these days, notably those made from hearts of palm, edamame, or konjac. I found that the long white daikon radish (mooli)

makes outstanding noodles, which I use in my **Pad Thai with Seared Tofu** (page 70). A spiralizer would be a good investment for this section so you can make your noodles fresh at home—I suggest a tabletop version.

You are welcome to use higher-carb options such as whole-grain or lentil pasta, if you prefer; just cook them per the package directions. But once you've tried my **Saag Lasagna** (page 62) or **Chutney Ramen** (page 69), it won't be about the noodles anymore!

2–3 medium zucchini/courgettes
(1 lb/450g)

1½ tsp salt, divided, plus more for
sprinkling zucchini

1 Tbsp ghee, or butter

1 tsp cumin seeds

1½ cups/240g diced onion

1 Indian green chile, jalapeño pepper,
or Thai chile, chopped

1 Tbsp grated ginger

1 Tbsp minced garlic

1 cup/240ml water

1 lb/450g fresh spinach, if frozen
thawed

1 tsp garam masala

15 oz/425g whole-milk ricotta

½ tsp cracked black pepper

2 oz/56g grated low-moisture
mozzarella

> **TO VEGANIZE**
>
> Use **Vegan Béchamel
> Sauce** (page 185) instead
> of the ricotta and use
> nutritional yeast or vegan
> cheese for topping in place
> of the mozzarella.

Saag Lasagna

SERVES: 4

Here I replace the traditional meat sauce with a glorious spinach
gravy that I typically use for saag paneer, and use ricotta for simplicity
instead of the béchamel. This is a rich, unique dish that will rightly
take center stage at every dinner party. Be warned that this dish will be
saucier than a traditional lasagna due to the water the zucchini gives
off. You can soak the sauce up using a slice of toasted **Zucchini Bread**
(page 14). In the photo the recipe was doubled and baked in a 9-x-13 in
baking dish, which is great for a crowd.

Step 1. Slice the zucchini lengthwise into ¹⁄₁₆ in/1.5-mm-thick slices
using a mandoline slicer or knife. (Be very careful while using a
mandoline; always use cut-resistant gloves.) Place the zucchini in
a colander over a bowl, sprinkle it lightly with salt, and set aside for
15–20 minutes to draw out the moisture as you make the saag.

Step 2. Preheat the oven to 400°F/200°C. Heat the ghee in a
medium saucepan over medium heat. When hot, add the cumin
seeds and wait until they are aromatic, then add the onions.
Increase the heat to medium-high, and cook, stirring occasionally,
until golden brown and caramelized.

Step 3. Lower the heat to medium, add the green chile, ginger, and
garlic, and sauté for 30 seconds. Pour in the water and bring to a boil.
Mix in the spinach gradually and cook until it just wilts. Add the garam
masala and 1 teaspoon salt and mix well. Turn off the stove and use an
immersion blender to blend the spinach mixture until smooth.

Step 4. Mix the ricotta, remaining ½ teaspoon of salt, and the pepper
well in a bowl and set aside. Pat the zucchini slices dry with paper towels.

Step 5. To assemble, in an 8-x-8-x-1 ½ in/20-x-20-x-4-cm baking pan
or casserole dish, layer one-third of the spinach saag, one-third of
the zucchini slices, and half the ricotta. Repeat. Top the last layer
of ricotta with the remaining spinach saag and zucchini slices, and
sprinkle mozzarella evenly on top.

Step 6. Bake for 40–45 minutes, or until the cheese melts and turns
golden brown in spots. Serve hot.

COOKING NOTES

Freeze leftovers in an airtight container for up to 2 months. Defrost in
the microwave.

17g protein
68 kcal

19g fat
171 kcal

323
CALORIES
PER SERVING

21g carbs
(5g fiber)
84 kcal

MINCED TOFU

6 oz/168g extra-firm tofu

2 tsp toasted sesame oil

4–5 medium scallions (2 oz/55g), sliced and divided into white and green parts

1 tsp tamari, or 2 tsp soy sauce

1 tsp Chinese 5-spice powder

1 tsp ground cumin

⅛ tsp cayenne

1 cup/30g fresh spinach or other greens of choice

SAUCE

½ cup/120ml heated low-sodium vegetable broth or hot water

2 Tbsp peanut butter, no sugar or additional oil added

2 Tbsp tamari, or ¼ cup soy sauce

2 Tbsp Sichuan chile oil (including the red pepper flakes), plus more as needed (see notes)

1 tsp. Chinkiang vinegar or rice vinegar

2 tsp minced garlic

½ tsp ground Sichuan peppercorns (see notes)

1 lb/450g veggie noodles of choice (I used hearts of palm noodles)

Dan Dan Noodles

SERVES: 2

When my spice-loving taste buds met a tingly Sichuan peppercorn at a potluck in college, they fell in love. A fiery snack sold on the streets of Sichuan, normally this dish will have minced pork though here I create a flavorful minced tofu that works seamlessly for the topping. A friend tipped me off about the easy substitution of peanut butter for Chinese sesame paste. Add an extra tablespoon of Sichuan chile oil to your bowl, it will be worth your while!

Step 1. To make the minced tofu, press the tofu on a flat surface between paper napkins to squeeze out any excess water. Finely crumble the tofu using your hands. Heat a small frying pan over medium-low heat. Add the oil, the white parts of the scallions, and tofu and cook, stirring, for 4–5 minutes, or until the tofu is dry. Add the tamari, Chinese 5-spice powder, cumin, and cayenne, mix well, and cook for 2–3 minutes, until the flavors meld together. Set aside.

Step 2. Bring a pot of salted water to a boil, add the spinach, and cook until bright green and just wilted. Drain and rinse with cold water immediately.

Step 3. Whisk all the ingredients for the sauce together in a bowl.

Step 4. Divide the noodles between two bowls. Spoon the sauce into each bowl and top with the minced tofu and spinach. You may want to warm the fully-assembled bowls up for a minute in the microwave prior to serving. Garnish with the green parts of the scallions and serve.

COOKING NOTES

To make a substitute for the Sichuan chile oil, heat a small saucepan over medium heat. Add 2 Tbsp neutral oil with a high smoke point, like avocado oil, along with 2 tsp gochugaru (Korean chile flakes that are more widely available), 1 bay leaf, a 1 inch stick of cinnamon, a ½ inch piece of ginger, and 1 star anise, if you have it. Cook, stirring, for about 1 minute, or until the oil simmers and the spices are fragrant. Let cool for 5 minutes, remove the bay leaf, cinnamon, ginger, and star anise, and use as directed in the recipe.

If you don't have ground Sichuan peppercorns on hand, you can substitute ½ tsp cracked black pepper plus ½ tsp ground coriander seed. Thanks to The Kitchn for this tip!

28g fat
252 kcal

18g protein
72 kcal

404
CALORIES
PER SERVING

20g carbs
(7g fiber)
80 kcal

2 medium zucchini/courgettes
(14 oz/400g total)

Salt, for sprinkling

PICO DE GALLO

1 medium plum or Roma tomato
(4 oz/110g), finely chopped

2 Tbsp finely chopped onion

2 Tbsp finely chopped cilantro/fresh
coriander

1 Tbsp lemon juice

½ tsp fine sea salt

AVOCADO SAUCE

1 medium avocado (7 oz/200g),
scooped

¼ cup/40g roughly chopped onion

1 small jalapeño pepper (see cooking
notes)

1 small bunch cilantro/fresh
coriander (1 oz/25g)

2 cloves garlic

2 Tbsp lemon juice

½ tsp salt

½ can black beans (7 oz/200g),
rinsed (see notes)

Avocado Pasta

SERVES: 2

My avocado pasta is a cold summer dish bursting with fresh Mexican flavors that could alternatively be considered a salad. We bring together traditional guacamole ingredients to make a creamy but spicy sauce and toss it with zucchini noodles, black beans, and fresh pico de gallo. You are unlikely to have leftover sauce, but if you do, use it as a dip or for **Avocado Toast** (page 20)!

Step 1. Spiralize the zucchini into the desired size (I like spaghetti-size noodles for this pasta). Place in a colander over a bowl, salt lightly, and let sit for 15–20 minutes to draw out the moisture. Alternatively, if you prefer an al dente texture, skip this step and spiralize right before serving to avoid having the noodles sit too long.

Step 2. Mix all the ingredients for the pico de gallo in a bowl and refrigerate.

Step 3. Blend all the ingredients for the avocado sauce in a food processor or blender until smooth, adding 1–2 tablespoons water if needed.

Step 4. Pat the zucchini noodles dry with a paper napkin. Add the black beans and avocado sauce and toss to combine.

Step 5. Garnish with pico de gallo and serve.

NOTES

If making your own black beans, use ¼ cup/40g dried beans.

For a less spicy sauce, seed the jalapeño before adding it to the blender.

Store the avocado sauce refrigerated in an airtight container for up to 2 days. Squeezing a lemon over the top will help reduce oxidation and keep the top layer from turning brown. If it bothers you, you can also simply skim off the top layer to reveal fresher-looking sauce below.

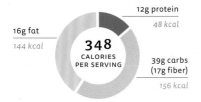

16g fat
144 kcal

12g protein
48 kcal

348
CALORIES
PER SERVING

39g carbs
(17g fiber)
156 kcal

1 Tbsp avocado oil

1 Tbsp + 1 tsp minced garlic, divided

1 Tbsp grated ginger

4–5 scallions, sliced and divided into white and green parts

1 cup/100g sliced white mushrooms

1 Tbsp spicy chutney of choice, such tomato or cilantro/fresh coriander, or sambal oelek or chile garlic sauce

1 Tbsp light sweet (yellow) miso (or red miso for a heavier taste)

1 Tbsp rice vinegar or white vinegar

1 Tbsp tamari or 2 Tbsp soy sauce

4 cups/960ml low-sodium vegetable broth or water

1 cup/100g mung bean sprouts

½ block (6 oz/168g) firm tofu , cut into ¾ inch/2-cm cubes

2 cups/60g spinach

1 tsp toasted sesame oil

4 baby bok choy (1 lb/450g), halved lengthwise

1 lb/450g veggie noodles of choice (I used hearts of palm noodles)

⅓ cup/50g sliced red bell pepper/ capsicum, cut into matchsticks

1 small jalapeño pepper, sliced

Chutney Ramen

SERVES: 2

This was inspired by the fiery ramen I had in Tokyo a few years ago, after navigating the labyrinth that is the Tokyo subway station. Always a fan of spicy food, I had a lightbulb moment when I realized other spicy sauces could probably be used to flavor the base as well. Thus, Chutney Ramen was born! I have experimented with a tomato chutney and a coriander (cilantro) chutney with great results, and you can also always fall back on a basic chile garlic sauce. Just try not to use a chutney that has a lot of coconut. I prefer this vegan, but feel free to add soft-boiled eggs to ramp up the umami of this dish.

Step 1. Heat the avocado oil in a large saucepan over medium heat. Add 1 Tbsp. of garlic, the ginger, and the white parts of the scallions and cook, stirring once or twice, for 2 minutes. Add the mushrooms, chutney, and miso paste, mix well, and cook for 2–3 minutes. Add the rice vinegar and tamari and cook for another minute.

Step 2. Add the broth and bring to a boil. Add the bean sprouts and cook until blanched, 2 minutes. Add the tofu and cook for another minute. Add the spinach, mix well, and turn off the stove to let the spinach cook in the residual heat.

Step 3. Heat the sesame oil in a medium sauté pan over medium-low heat. Add the remaining 1 teaspoon garlic and sauté for 1 minute. Place the baby bok choy cut-side down in the pan and cook, covered, until both sides are lightly browned, 4–6 minutes, turning halfway. You can add 1–2 tablespoons water to deglaze the pan if needed.

Step 4. Divide the veggie noodles between two bowls. Pour the broth over the noodles and top with the bok choy. Garnish each serving with the green parts of the scallions, the bell pepper, and jalapeño and serve.

COOKING NOTES

This recipe moves fast, so have all ingredients ready before starting!

21g protein
84 kcal

15g fat
135 kcal

351
CALORIES
PER SERVING

33g carbs
(9g fiber)
132 kcal

2 Tbsp low-sodium vegetable broth or hot water

4 tsp chile garlic paste, (such as Huy Fong)

2 tsp tamari, or 4 tsp soy sauce

2 tsp store-bought tamarind concentrate paste, such as Tamicon, or 4 tsp fresh tamarind paste (page 184)

2 tsp maple syrup

1 medium daikon radish (12 oz/340g), peeled and spiralized to fettucine size

¼ block (3 oz/84g) extra-firm tofu

6 tsp toasted sesame oil, divided

1 small red bell pepper/capsicum (4 oz/110g), spiralized or cut into matchsticks

1 heaping cup/100g shredded purple cabbage

1 Tbsp minced garlic

4–5 chopped scallions, divided into white and green parts

4 Tbsp/28g finely chopped dry-roasted unsalted peanuts, divided

Salt

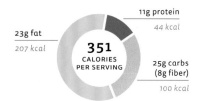

23g fat
207 kcal

351
CALORIES
PER SERVING

11g protein
44 kcal

25g carbs
(8g fiber)
100 kcal

Pad Thai with Seared Tofu

SERVES: 2

Ten years ago, I had the best pad Thai ever in Vegas, of all places! Since then, I have tried endless variations of the sauce to try and live up to that memory, until I developed this spicy version that I love. In search of a substitute for rice noodles, I chanced upon Ali Mafucci's book *Inspiralized*, which suggested daikon radish (mooli) as a candidate to be spiralized. And voila! When boiled until tender, daikon becomes translucent and makes a wonderful carrier for the tangy sauce and chopped peanuts.

Step 1. To make the sauce, combine the broth, chile garlic paste, tamari, tamarind paste, and maple syrup in a small bowl and stir to mix. Set aside.

Step 2. Bring a pot of salted water to a boil and add the radish noodles. Cook for 8–10 minutes or until tender. Drain and rinse with cold water. Set aside.

Step 3. Slice the tofu into roughly 1 x ¾ in/2.5 x 2cm rectangles. Place them on a paper towel, place another paper towel on top, and press down gently to release as much moisture as possible. Heat a large pan over medium-high heat and add 2 teaspoons of oil. Add the tofu and cook for 5–7 minutes on one side. When you see the bottom browning, carefully turn the tofu over and cook on the other side for 3–4 minutes. Transfer to a paper towel–lined plate.

Step 4. In the same pan, sauté the bell pepper in 1 teaspoon oil over medium-high heat for 2 minutes, until tender but still crisp. Transfer to a plate. Add another teaspoon of oil and the cabbage, and sauté for 2 minutes. Transfer to the plate. Add the remaining 2 teaspoons of oil, the garlic, and the white parts of the scallions, reduce the heat to medium, and sauté for 1 minute. Add the radish noodles and cook for another minute or two.

Step 5. Add the cabbage, bell pepper, tofu, 3 tablespoons chopped peanuts, and half the sauce and toss with tongs to mix and cook for about 2 more minutes until heated through. Add more sauce as desired and sprinkle with salt to taste. Garnish with the remaining 1 tablespoon of chopped peanuts and the green parts of the scallions and serve.

6 oz/168g paneer, thawed and riced or finely crumbled

3 Tbsp chickpea flour

½ tsp coarse or flaky sea salt

¼ tsp cracked black pepper

1 egg yolk

2 tsp cornstarch/cornflour, divided

GREEN PEA PESTO

¼ cup/40g frozen green peas, thawed

1 medium bunch (1 oz/28g) fresh basil

2 medium cloves garlic

2 Tbsp raw cashews

¼ tsp cracked black pepper

¼ tsp fine sea salt

1½ Tbsp olive oil

2 tsp lemon juice, as needed (start with 1 tsp and add more to taste)

1 Tbsp olive oil

Pesto Paneer Gnocchi

SERVES: 3

I was inspired to create this high-protein version after watching a video of Jamie Oliver's Italian food guru, Gennaro Contaldo, making traditional potato gnocchi. Don't let homemade gnocchi intimidate you—this is one of those experiments that turns out perfectly the first time. It is served with a lovely pesto that has a touch of sweetness from the peas and bright acidity from the lemon.

Step 1. On a flat surface lined with parchment paper, combine the paneer, flour, salt, pepper, and egg yolk. Mix with your hands and knead just enough to incorporate all the ingredients into a ball. The dough will be sticky.

Step 2. Dust a fresh sheet of parchment paper with 1 teaspoon cornstarch. Transfer the dough to the paper and gently roll around to coat with the cornstarch, until the dough is not sticky anymore. Slice into 8 pieces with a sharp knife.

Step 3. Using both your hands like a rolling pin, roll each piece into a long pipe about ¾ in/2cm in diameter. You can squeeze and shape the pipes as needed. Cut each pipe into ¾ in/2-cm pieces with a sharp knife. If desired, dip the back of a fork's tines into the remaining 1 teaspoon of cornstarch and press gently on each piece to get striped indentations.

Step 4. Bring a pot of salted water to a boil. Working in batches, drop the gnocchi in the boiling water and let cook until they rise to the top, about 2 minutes. Do not overcook. Remove with a slotted spoon and transfer to a plate to dry.

Step 5. Blend all the pesto ingredients together in a small food processor, adding 1 teaspoon of water if needed.

Step 6. Heat the olive oil in a medium sauté pan over medium heat. When hot, add the gnocchi. Cook, flipping until golden brown on both sides, 2–3 minutes. Add the pesto and toss to coat. Cook until heated through and serve immediately.

COOKING NOTES

You can freeze uncooked gnocchi (prepared through Step 3) for up to 2 months. Freeze in a container or plate large enough that the pieces don't touch each other for the first few hours; bag them after they are frozen. Cook from frozen as described in Step 4.

30g fat
270 kcal

382
CALORIES
PER SERVING

16g protein
64 kcal

12g carbs
(2g fiber)
48 kcal

1 tsp cornstarch/cornflour

1 tsp + ¼ cup/60ml water, divided

2 Tbsp butter

1 lb/450g veggie noodles of choice
(see notes)

¾ scant cup/78g grated pecorino
romano (or Parmesan cheese, if you
can't find vegetarian pecorino)

¼ heaping cup/34g grated Parmesan
cheese

2 tsp cracked black pepper

Salt to taste

Cacio e Pepe

SERVES: 2

Few dishes are as fast and spectacular as this Roman superstar, cacio e pepe. We take a clever (if I may say so myself) shortcut to starchy pasta water by using a cornstarch slurry. Combined with butter, cheeses, and pepper, it creates a dreamy sauce that clings to veggie noodles and satisfies every craving. The ratio of 70/30 for the pecorino and Parmesan cheeses comes to you from Stanley Tucci's show, *Searching for Italy*. The vegan version of this dish may be unexpected but proudly holds its own, using a thick, creamy béchamel sauce combined with nutritional yeast for maximum flavor.

Step 1. Combine the cornstarch and 1 teaspoon of water in a small bowl and mix well to make a slurry. Set aside.

Step 2. Heat the butter in a medium sauté pan over medium heat. When it melts, add the noodles and mix to coat. Add the remaining ¼ cup/60ml of water (see cooking notes) and the cornstarch slurry and mix well. Add both cheeses and pepper and cook, stirring continuously, to make a thick, creamy sauce that coats the noodles, adding more water as needed 1 tablespoon at a time, for 5–10 minutes. Taste and add salt, if desired (the cheeses are quite salty). Serve immediately.

COOKING NOTES

For the veggie noodles, I used those made of hearts of palm that look like bucatini. Spiralize to one size thicker than spaghetti if making your own.

If using zucchini noodles, you don't need to add water in Step 2. The zoodles will release water that can be used for this step. You can let most of the water cook off so you are left with a creamy sauce. Alternatively, if you prefer an al dente texture, add the zoodles at the end and use ¼ cup/60ml water in Step 2.

28g fat
252 kcal

19g protein
76 kcal

388
CALORIES
PER SERVING

15g carbs
(2g fiber)
60 kcal

3 Tbsp olive oil

1 small onion (4 oz/110g), finely diced

2 small carrots (4 oz/110g), finely diced

2 medium stalks celery (3 oz/80g), finely diced

1 bay leaf

1 small bell pepper/capsicum (4 oz/110g), finely diced

1 cup/100g finely diced white mushrooms, or porcini if you prefer a meatier flavor

1½ Tbsp minced garlic

1 tsp grated ginger

1 tsp garam masala

¾ tsp red chile flakes

½ tsp ground cumin

½ tsp ground coriander seed

1 (15-oz/400-g) can diced tomatoes

2 cups/480ml low-sodium vegetable broth or water

¾ cup/90g dried green or brown lentils

½ tsp salt

½ tsp cracked black pepper

1 lb/450g veggie noodles of choice (I used zucchini noodles)

2 Tbsp chopped fresh Italian parsley, for garnish

Curried Lentil Mushroom Bolognese

SERVES: 3

Lentils and mushrooms form the hearty base of this "bolognese" (traditionally an Italian meat sauce), and a curried flavor gives it a little twist. It makes a quick and easy weeknight dinner. Often, I will serve leftover sauce over cauliflower rice for the next day's lunch.

Step 1. Spiralize the zucchini into the desired size (I like spaghetti-size noodles for this pasta). Place in a colander over a bowl, salt lightly, and let sit for 15–20 minutes to draw out the moisture. Alternatively, if you prefer an al dente texture, skip this step and spiralize right before serving to avoid having the noodles sit too long.

Step 2. Heat a medium saucepan over medium heat. Add the oil, onion, carrots, celery, and bay leaf and cook, stirring, until the carrots are tender, 15–20 minutes. Add the bell pepper and mushrooms and cook for 3–4 minutes. Add the garlic, ginger, garam masala, chile flakes, cumin, and coriander and cook for 1 minute. Deglaze the pan with 1 tablespoon of water if needed. Add the tomatoes, mix, and cook, covered, until well combined, about 5 minutes.

Step 3. Add the broth, lentils, salt, and pepper and bring to a boil. Cover and simmer until the lentils are fully cooked, 20–30 minutes. Season with salt and pepper to taste.

Step 4. Pat the zucchini noodles dry with a paper napkin. Divide the noodles among four bowls. Top with the sauce, garnish with parsley, and serve.

15g fat
135 kcal

12g protein
48 kcal

347
CALORIES
PER SERVING

41g carbs
(9g fiber)
164 kcal

2 medium zucchini/courgettes (14 oz/400g total), spiralized to pappardelle size

1 (6 oz/168g) block feta, or crumbled feta (see note)

1 lb/450g grape or cherry tomatoes

2 Tbsp olive oil

2 Tbsp minced garlic

½ tsp fine sea salt, plus more for sprinkling zucchini

½ tsp cracked black pepper

1 tsp cornstarch/cornflour

2 Tbsp + 1 tsp water, divided

TO VEGANIZE
Use vegan feta.

Feta Pasta

SERVES: 4

This "uunifetapasta" recipe created by a Finnish blogger went viral on TikTok at some point during the pandemic, and I lost no time in creating a low-carb version. It's easy, delicious, and filling—burst grape tomatoes work wonderfully well with tangy feta, and the zucchini lends a much-needed touch of lightness to this dish.

Step 1. Place the zucchini in a colander over a bowl, salt the noodles lightly to draw out moisture, and set aside for 10–15 minutes. Preheat the oven to 400°F/200°C.

Step 2. Place the feta block in the center of an 8-x-8-x-1 ½ in/20-x-20-x-4-cm baking pan or casserole dish. Surround with the tomatoes and drizzle with olive oil. Sprinkle the tomatoes with garlic, salt, and pepper and stir to mix.

Step 3. Bake for 35 minutes, or until the top of the feta starts to turn golden brown and the tomatoes burst.

Step 4. Using the back of a spoon, mash the feta to break it up and stir to combine with the tomatoes. Combine the cornstarch with 1 teaspoon of water to make a slurry. Add the slurry and remaining 2 tablespoons of water to the baking pan and mix well to make a creamy sauce.

Step 5. Add the zoodles and toss to coat with the sauce. Garnish with additional salt and pepper to taste and serve.

COOKING NOTES

If using crumbled feta, use your hands to press it into a block shape in the center of the dish in Step 2.

Cubed eggplant would make a wonderful addition to this dish. Add it in with the tomatoes in Step 2.

8g protein
32 kcal

13g fat
117 kcal

189
CALORIES
PER SERVING

10g carbs
(2g fiber)
40 kcal

4 cups/400g small cauliflower florets

ONION-TOMATO SAUCE

2 Tbsp ghee or butter

1½ cups/225g diced onion

1½ Tbsp grated ginger

1½ Tbsp minced garlic

3 cups/450g diced tomatoes, or
1 (15-oz/400-g) can diced tomatoes

½ cup/56g raw cashews, soaked in
hot water for 15 minutes and drained

1½ tsp salt

1 tsp cracked black pepper

1 tsp garam masala

4 oz/112g paneer, thawed if frozen,
cubed

¼ cup/60ml heavy cream/double
cream (optional)

½ cup/56g grated low-moisture
mozzarella

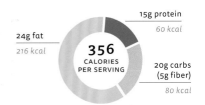

24g fat
216 kcal

15g protein
60 kcal

356
CALORIES
PER SERVING

20g carbs
(5g fiber)
80 kcal

Paneer Mac-Khani and Cheese

SERVES: 4

This is an indulgent and crave-worthy dish that was inspired by Aroqa, one of my favorite Indian restaurants in Manhattan. Cauliflower "pasta" is studded with paneer in a creamy onion-tomato sauce, with a sprinkle of mozzarella on top for good measure. I don't know a lot of people that can say no to this one. Serve with a slice of **Zucchini Bread** (page 14) rubbed with garlic and toasted with butter.

Step 1. Preheat the oven to 350°F/180°C.

Step 2. Bring a medium saucepan of salted water to a boil. Add the cauliflower florets, and cook until tender, 5–10 minutes. Drain, rinse, and set aside.

Step 3. Meanwhile, to make the onion-tomato sauce, heat the same saucepan over medium-high heat. When hot, add the ghee and onions and cook, stirring occasionally, until the onions are golden brown and caramelized, about 5 minutes. Add the ginger and garlic and cook for 1 minute. Add all the remaining sauce ingredients, mix well, cover, and cook until the tomatoes break down into a thick paste and start oozing, 5–6 minutes. Deglaze the pan with 1 tablespoon of water if needed. Blend until smooth with an immersion blender.

Step 4. Add the cauliflower and paneer to the pan with the onion-tomato sauce. Add the heavy cream, if using. Season with salt and pepper to taste.

Step 5. Pour into an 8-x-8-x-1 ½ in/20-x-20-x-4-cm baking dish. Top with grated cheese, and bake for 20–30 minutes, or until the cheese is lightly browned in spots. Serve hot.

COOKING NOTES

If you have panko breadcrumbs made from my **Zucchini Bread** (page 14), sprinkle on top with the cheese in Step 5 for some bonus texture!

SALADS

Salads are such a stereotypical notion of vegetarian food that I almost didn't want to include a salad section in this book. Too many restaurant salads are prepared with little thought and the same old laundry list of ingredients; I find them uninspiring and used to dread chewing them mindlessly in front of my computer (as I often did in the office).

The salads in this section, though, are quite unlike any you may have had before. They feature hearty and delicious toppings such as falafel and marinated paneer sitting on a bed of vegetables, and take inspiration from around the world, like the homely sundal of South India or the prettiest caprese from Italy. My **Cucumber Papdi Chaat** (page 84) is so much fun that it barely qualifies as a salad. You will be delighted by the variety, flavor, and sheer joyfulness of these dishes, and salads will never feel like a punishment again.

MASALA PEANUTS

1 Tbsp chickpea flour

2 tsp water

1 tsp avocado oil

1 tsp paprika

¼ tsp salt

¼ tsp ground cumin

¼ tsp cracked black pepper

¼ tsp ground turmeric

¼ cup/28g raw skinned peanuts, or cashews or skinned almonds

CHAAT

¾ cup/170g whole-milk plain Greek yogurt or dairy-free yogurt

1–2 Tbsp water

¾ cup/100g canned or cooked chickpeas, drained

¼ tsp salt

⅛ tsp cayenne

3 baby cucumbers, or 1 large cucumber (11 oz/300g), sliced into disks ¹⁄₁₆ in/2mm thick

2 Tbsp tamarind-date chutney (such as Swad)

1½ Tbsp cilantro/fresh coriander chutney (such as Swad)

½ cup/90g finely chopped tomatoes

¼ cup/40g finely chopped onion

2 Tbsp finely chopped cilantro/fresh coriander

1 tsp chaat masala (optional)

Cucumber Papdi Chaat

SERVES: 2 *as a main*

Craving chaat? My twist on this iconic Indian street food dish uses cucumber slices as papdi (crispy deep-fried flour-based rounds). Layered with creamy Greek yogurt and spiced chickpeas, and topped with tangy chutneys and crispy masala peanuts, this makes an easy, refreshing, and delicious summer lunch.

Step 1. Preheat the air fryer to 350°F/180°C or oven to 400°F/200°C.

Step 2. Mix together all the ingredients for masala peanuts, except the peanuts, in a bowl. Add the peanuts and mix until they are coated with the paste. Lightly spray an air fryer base with oil and spread the nut mixture evenly on the base. Air fry for 5 minutes, tossing halfway through. If using the oven, spread the peanuts evenly on a baking sheet lined with parchment paper (you can also lightly spray the parchment) and bake for 12–15 minutes, until golden brown, turning over halfway through (you may need to use a spoon to scrape the peanut mixture off the parchment). Remove from the air fryer or oven and let cool. Finely chop or pulse the peanuts 3–4 times in a food processor and set aside.

Step 3. Whip the yogurt in a bowl with just enough water to make it spreadable. In a separate bowl, mix the chickpeas with salt and cayenne.

Step 4. Layer half the cucumber slices, chickpeas, and yogurt on a plate. Drizzle half the tamarind-date chutney and coriander chutney over the top. Sprinkle with half the tomato, onion, and masala peanuts on top. Repeat to assemble the second plate. Garnish with cilantro and chaat masala, and serve.

COOKING NOTES

Double the recipe for masala peanuts. You can store them in an airtight container in the freezer for up to 4 months. In a pinch, use any salted or spiced nuts in place of the masala peanuts.

18g protein
72 kcal

17g fat
153 kcal

365
CALORIES
PER SERVING

35g carbs
(8g fiber)
140 kcal

FALAFEL

1 cup/100g roughly chopped scallions (both white and green parts)

½ heaping cup/100g dried chickpeas, soaked overnight and rinsed

Packed ½ cup/15g chopped cilantro/fresh coriander

Packed ½ cup/15g chopped Italian parsley

8–10 fresh mint leaves

2 medium cloves garlic

2 Tbsp avocado oil

1 Tbsp chickpea flour

1½ tsp ground cumin

1 tsp ground coriander seed

¾ tsp salt

½ tsp cayenne

¼ tsp baking powder

GREEK YOGURT DRESSING

⅓ cup/70g whole-milk plain Greek yogurt or non-dairy yogurt

1 small clove garlic, minced

1–2 Tbsp water

¾ tsp lemon juice

½ tsp olive oil

¼ tsp fine sea salt

¼ tsp cracked black pepper

2 cups/300g chopped salad vegetables (greens, tomatoes, onions, cucumber)

2 tsp harissa or hot sauce (optional)

Falafel Salad

SERVES: 2   *as a main*

The best falafel I ever had was in the vibrant bylanes of Le Marais in Paris, after standing in line for an hour. After years of trial and error, this attempt gets dangerously close to that flavor without deep-frying! The trick is to blend in the oil with the falafel mixture instead of spraying it on the outside. You can use the air fryer or the oven to get perfect falafel, crispy on the outside, moist and fluffy on the inside.

Step 1. Combine all the ingredients for falafel except the baking powder in a food processor and blend to a coarse mixture (the texture of sand), scraping down the sides often. Chill in the refrigerator for 30 minutes.

Step 2. Preheat the air fryer to 375°F/190°C or the oven to 425°F/220°C. Lightly spray the base of the air fryer with oil, or spray a baking sheet. (I use an avocado oil spray.)

Step 3. Take the falafel mixture out and stir in the baking powder. Shape the falafel into tablespoon-sized balls and place in the air fryer or on the baking sheet, with room between the balls. (You should have 12–14 falafels.) Spray oil lightly over the falafel balls if desired.

Step 4. Air fry for 15–18 minutes undisturbed, or bake for 20–25 minutes, flipping halfway through. (Oven-baked falafels may not brown as evenly, but will still taste great). While the falafel bakes, mix together all the ingredients for the Greek yogurt dressing and refrigerate.

Step 5. Toss the falafel with the salad vegetables, drizzle with yogurt dressing and harissa, if using, and serve immediately.

COOKING NOTES

It's important to use dried chickpeas for this recipe. Do not use canned or cooked chickpeas, as the falafel may come apart easily.

You can add a little more chickpea flour to the batter if it seems watery and hard to shape.

You can prepare the falafel mixture ahead and store in an airtight container for a week in the fridge, or up to 2 months in the freezer. Defrost at room temperature for 4–5 hours or overnight.

16g protein
64 kcal

20g fat
180 kcal

420 CALORIES PER SERVING

44g carbs (9g fiber)
176 kcal

5 oz/140g fresh mozzarella, sliced

2–3 heirloom tomatoes (11 oz/300g), or plum, Roma, or beefsteak tomatoes, at room temperature

4–5 leaves fresh basil

1 Tbsp extra-virgin olive oil

¼ tsp coarse or flaky sea salt

Caprese Salad

SERVES: 4 *as a side*

The simplest ingredients often make the most sumptuous of dishes. For a recipe where the whole is so much greater than the sum of its parts, look no further than this salad from the gorgeous island of Capri. Use high-quality ingredients—organic tomatoes in peak summer, extra-virgin olive oil, and flaky salt such as Maldon—they really *make* this salad. Sometimes I will make a mini version with cherry or grape tomatoes and mini mozzarella balls, or even skewer them for a fun appetizer.

Step 1. Arrange the mozzarella and tomato slices on a plate and top with basil.

Step 2. Drizzle the olive oil over the top, garnish with sea salt, and serve.

COOKING NOTES

You can substitute pesto if you do not have fresh basil.

If desired, drizzle a few drops of balsamic vinegar over the salad before serving.

9g protein
36 kcal

11g fat
99 kcal

151
CALORIES
PER SERVING

4g carbs
(1g fiber)
16 kcal

¼ cup/55g whole-milk plain Greek yogurt

1 tsp rice vinegar or white vinegar

1 tsp Dijon mustard

¼ tsp salt

¼ tsp cracked black pepper

1 small green apple such as Granny Smith (5 oz/140g), diced

¾ cup/75g thinly sliced celery

½ cup/56g toasted walnuts, chopped

½ oz/14g shaved Parmesan cheese, shaved using a vegetable peeler

½ scant cup/50g raspberries

TO VEGANIZE

Use your preferred vegan Greek-style yogurt in place of the Greek yogurt and skip the Parmesan.

Waldorf Salad

SERVES: 4 *as a side*

Waldorf salad is a timeless classic originally created by the Waldorf Astoria Hotel in New York City. Apples, celery, grapes, and walnuts are the stars of this delicately sweet and lightly tart salad, tossed in mayo. My version uses raspberries, which are low in sugar, instead of grapes, a creamy Greek yogurt mayo, and some shaved Parmesan for added protein and texture.

Step 1. Blend together all the ingredients for the mayo.

Step 2. Combine the apple, celery, and walnuts in a bowl. Add the mayo and toss, adding more salt and pepper as needed. Refrigerate until ready to serve.

Step 3. Garnish with the shaved Parmesan and raspberries immediately before serving.

COOKING NOTES

To prevent the diced apples browning, submerge them in a bowl of water with a dash of lemon juice until ready to mix with the mayo.

Serve the salad on a bed of lettuce, if desired.

11g fat
99 kcal

5g protein
20 kcal

159
CALORIES
PER SERVING

10g carbs
(3g fiber)
40 kcal

DRESSING

1 Tbsp olive oil

1 Tbsp lemon juice

1 tsp red wine vinegar

½ tsp dried oregano

½ tsp fine sea salt

½ tsp cracked black pepper

2 oz/56g block feta, diced

1 large (or 3 baby) cucumbers
(11 oz/300g), sliced into discs and
halved

⅔ cup/100g grape tomatoes, halved
lengthwise

⅓ cup/50g diced green bell pepper/
capsicum

⅓ cup/50g thinly sliced red onion

8–10 kalamata olives (1½ oz/40g),
pitted and sliced

TO VEGANIZE
Use half a (15 oz/400g) can
of drained chickpeas in
place of the feta.

Greek Salad

SERVES: 2 *as a side*

Here is a Mediterranean classic that always takes me to the sea. With tangy feta and olives, refreshing cucumbers, sweet tomatoes, the crunch of bell pepper and onions, and a lift from red wine vinegar and lemon, all tossed in the best-quality olive oil you can find, this salad is all about balance.

Step 1. Whisk together all the ingredients for the dressing in a large bowl.

Step 2. Add the feta and all the vegetables to the bowl and toss until coated with the dressing. Refrigerate until ready to serve.

COOKING NOTE

For a heartier meal, add some whole-grain pasta and make this a pasta salad. You may need to increase the amount of dressing.

6g protein
24 kcal

15g fat
135 kcal

215
CALORIES
PER SERVING

14g carbs
(3g fiber)
56 kcal

1 heaping cup/200g dried chickpeas, soaked overnight, or 2 (15-oz/400-g) cans chickpeas, drained and rinsed

2 Tbsp avocado oil, or other neutral oil of choice

2 tsp black mustard seeds (yellow mustard seeds are less pungent, but will work as a substitute)

2 Indian green chiles, jalapeño peppers, or Thai chiles, chopped

10–15 fresh curry leaves, chopped, or 20–30 whole dried curry leaves, crumbled

½ tsp urad dal (black gram, split and skinned; optional)

¼ tsp asafoetida (hing, sometimes called yellow powder)

½ cup/75g finely diced onion

1½ tsp salt

3 Tbsp fresh or frozen shredded coconut, or dry unsweetened shredded coconut

1 Tbsp lemon juice

Sundal

SERVES: 4 *as a side*

My favorite part about the Hindu festival of Navaratri (nine nights) is, unsurprisingly, the food. Sundal is a dry stir-fry (and a specialty of my dad's) made with an array of different legumes such as chickpeas or whole green moong. The simple tadka of mustard seeds, green chile, curry leaves, hing, and coconut instantly elevates this dish and, in my humble opinion, represents the essence of South Indian home cooking.

Step 1. If using dried chickpeas, combine them with 3 cups/720ml of water in a pressure cooker and cook just until done (about 7 minutes on high in an Instant Pot; quick release pressure after 5 minutes). The beans should be cooked but crunchy. Skip this step if using canned chickpeas.

Step 2. Heat a medium sauté pan over medium-high heat. When hot, add the oil and mustard seeds. When the mustard seeds pop, turn the heat down to medium and add the chiles, curry leaves, urad dal, and asafoetida. Cook until the urad dal turns light golden brown, 1 minute.

Step 3. Add the onions and cook, stirring, until soft, 5–6 minutes.

Step 4. Add the chickpeas and salt, mix well, and cook for 2–3 minutes, until heated through. Do not overcook or they will get mushy.

Step 5. Turn off the stove, add the coconut and lemon juice, and mix well. Serve hot.

COOKING NOTES

In Step 1, it is OK for the chickpeas to be slightly al dente. They will cook for a couple of minutes longer in Step 4!

You can also serve this as a main, on a bed of greens.

11g protein
44 kcal

12g fat
108 kcal

296
CALORIES
PER SERVING

36g carbs
(8g fiber)
144 kcal

1 Tbsp olive oil

1 fennel bulb (4 oz/110g), sliced thinly lengthwise

1 (15-oz/400-g) can Great Northern beans, rinsed and drained

2 oz/55g arugula

¼ cup/28g shaved Parmesan cheese

LEMON AND CRISPY GARLIC VINAIGRETTE

1 Tbsp olive oil

1 tsp minced garlic

½ tsp fine sea salt

½ tsp cracked black pepper

¼ tsp dried oregano

1 Tbsp lemon juice

TO VEGANIZE

Use nutritional yeast instead of the Parmesan, or simply skip the cheese.

White Bean and Fennel Salad

SERVES: 4 *as a side*

Caramelized fennel and a tadka-style lemon and crispy garlic dressing take this simple and hearty bean salad to the next level, while arugula and shaved Parmesan add a pleasing interplay of texture.

Step 1. Heat a medium sauté pan over medium heat. When hot, add the oil and sliced fennel and cook, stirring, until lightly browned around the edges, 5–10 minutes. Transfer to a large bowl to cool.

Step 2. For the dressing, return the same pan to medium heat and add the oil. When hot, add the garlic—it will sizzle as it hits the oil. Let simmer until the tadka (tempering) is fragrant and the garlic is lightly browned, about 1 minute. Turn off the stove, add the salt, pepper, and oregano, and mix. Let cool for 5 minutes. Add the lemon juice and mix.

Step 3. Add the beans and dressing to the fennel in the large bowl and mix. Add the arugula and gently stir a couple of times to incorporate. Top with the shaved Parmesan and serve warm or chilled.

COOKING NOTES

You can also use cannellini beans or navy beans in this recipe. If using dried beans, use a heaping ½ cup/100g and cook until soft.

10g protein
40 kcal

9g fat
81 kcal

217
CALORIES
PER SERVING

24g carbs
(6g fiber)
96 kcal

PEANUT SAUCE

¼ cup/64g peanut butter, no sugar or additional oil added

¼ cup/60ml low-sodium vegetable broth or hot water, plus more as needed

4 tsp chile garlic paste, (such as Huy Fong)

2 tsp tamari or 4 tsp. soy sauce

2 tsp store-bought tamarind concentrate paste, such as Tamicon, or 4 tsp fresh tamarind paste (page 184)

2 tsp maple syrup

3 oz/84g tempeh or extra-firm tofu

2 tsp toasted sesame oil

2 eggs

20 green beans (4 oz/110g), ends trimmed

1 cup/100g mung bean sprouts

3 cups/100g fresh spinach

1 small red bell pepper/capsicum (4 oz/110g), sliced into thin strips lengthwise

¼ tsp fine sea salt

½ tsp cracked black pepper

TO VEGANIZE
Omit the eggs.

Gado-Gado

SERVES: 4   *as a light main or side*

I tried gado-gado at an Indonesian restaurant called the Bali Kitchen (sadly closed now) in NYC and was struck by the simple yet sumptuous platter—an array of cooked vegetables and proteins served with a spicy-sweet peanut sauce. Normally, it would have rice cakes and potato, along with vegetables and tempeh. Here I keep it low-carb by using an array of non-starchy vegetables.

Step 1. Whisk together all the ingredients for the peanut sauce in a bowl until smooth, adding more hot water or broth, 1 tablespoon at a time, as needed.

Step 2. Slice the tempeh into triangles with roughly 2 inch/5-cm sides. Heat a small skillet over medium-high heat. Add the sesame oil and the tempeh and cook on one side until visibly brown, 3–4 minutes, then flip to cook the other side. Remove from the heat and set aside.

Step 3. Place the eggs in a medium saucepan, fill with enough water to submerge, and bring to a rolling boil. Boil for 10–12 minutes. Turn off the stove, cover, and let sit for 10 minutes. Plunge the eggs into an ice bath, peel, and halve.

Step 4. Rinse the same saucepan, fill with salted water, and bring to a boil. Add the green beans and cook until bright green and soft, about 2 minutes. Use a slotted spoon to transfer the green beans to a plate. Add the bean sprouts to the boiling water and cook until just cooked through, about 2 minutes. Remove and transfer to a plate. Add the spinach and turn off the stove as soon as it turns bright green and wilts. Drain and rinse with cold water.

Step 5. Arrange all the ingredients including the red bell pepper on a large plate or platter. Drizzle with the peanut sauce, sprinkle with salt and pepper, and serve.

COOKING NOTES

The sauce will thicken as it cools. Warm it up in the microwave for a few seconds before serving, or add a little bit of hot water and mix.

Use any vegetables of your choice, such as broccoli, cauliflower, and so on, cooked until tender.

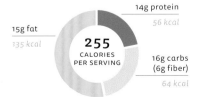

15g fat
135 kcal

255 CALORIES PER SERVING

14g protein
56 kcal

16g carbs (6g fiber)
64 kcal

½ cup/110g whole-milk plain Greek yogurt

1 Tbsp avocado oil, or other neutral oil of choice

1 Tbsp lemon juice

1 tsp grated ginger

1 tsp minced garlic

1 tsp paprika

1 tsp garam masala or chaat masala

½ tsp ground turmeric

6 oz/168g paneer, chopped into ¾ in/2-cm cubes

1 cup/150g chopped red bell pepper/capsicum, into ¾ in/2-cm pieces

1 cup/150g chopped green bell pepper/capsicum, into ¾ in/2-cm pieces

1 cup/150g chopped onion, chopped into ¾ in/2-cm pieces

1½ tsp avocado oil, or other neutral oil of choice

3 cups/90g fresh spinach, kale, or other greens of choice

MINT RAITA

¼ cup/55g whole-milk plain Greek yogurt

1 Tbsp water

6–8 fresh mint leaves

½ tsp ground cumin

Pinch of salt

¼ tsp cracked black pepper

Tandoori Paneer Salad

SERVES: 3 *as a main*

Few salads are as sumptuous as this one. Normally served as an appetizer, tandoori paneer usually involves skewering the marinated paneer and vegetables and grilling them in the oven (tandoor). This recipe simplifies the process and cooks the paneer on the stovetop, which also makes it less chewy. I serve it on a bed of greens with a creamy mint raita, for a completely un-salad-like experience that also gets in a whopping amount of protein.

Step 1. Whisk together all the ingredients for the marinade in a large bowl. Add the paneer, peppers, and onions and mix to coat each piece well with the marinade, using your hands if needed. Cover and refrigerate for 2–4 hours.

Step 2. Heat a medium sauté pan (preferably nonstick) over medium-high heat and spray with oil or cooking spray. Transfer the marinated mixture to the pan and cook, stirring occasionally, until the paneer is golden brown, 5–10 minutes. The marinade may stick to the pan a little; just scrape any bits off to deglaze the pan while stirring.

Step 3. Blend all the ingredients for the mint raita together in a bowl.

Step 4. Divide the spinach among three plates and serve the cooked paneer and vegetables on the bed of greens, drizzled with raita.

> **TO VEGANIZE**
> Use extra-firm tofu in place of the paneer, and your preferred plain vegan yogurt in place of the Greek yogurt for the marinade and raita. Marinate for 4–6 hours in Step 1.

19g protein
76 kcal

24g fat
216 kcal

356
CALORIES
PER SERVING

16g carbs
(3g fiber)
64 kcal

2–3 Yukon gold potatoes or radishes (12 oz/340g), peeled and diced

2 small carrots (4 oz/110g), peeled and diced

4 eggs

LEMON AIOLI

¾ cup/170g whole-milk plain Greek yogurt

1 Tbsp lemon juice

2 tsp olive oil

½ Tbsp lemon zest

1 tsp minced garlic

½ tsp fine sea salt

½ tsp cracked black pepper

1 cup/160g frozen green peas, defrosted

3 large or 6 small dill pickles (unsweetened), finely chopped

3 Tbsp chopped fresh dill

TO VEGANIZE
Replace the eggs with a 15 oz/400g can of drained chickpeas and use your preferred plain vegan yogurt in place of the Greek yogurt.

Olivier Salad

SERVES: 4   *as a light main or side*

This Russian salad is a hearty combination of boiled potatoes, eggs, peas, carrots, and dill pickles, usually dressed with creamy mayo. I first tried it at Mari Vanna, a charming Russian restaurant in NYC. My talented photographer and friend Alex, who is originally from Ukraine, says it is usually consumed alongside a night of merriment (that includes plenty of vodka), and therefore, the greasier the salad, the better! However, I steer you in a different direction in this book with a refreshing lemon aioli that sinks in even better the next day. For a more authentic taste, use **Greek Yogurt Mayo** (page 91) in place of the lemon aioli.

I don't use a lot of potato in this book, but I recommend it in this salad if you're going to chill it overnight. When cooked and cooled for several hours, potatoes build up resistant starch that functions like fiber in your body.

Step 1. Bring a large pot of salted water to a boil. Add the potatoes, carrots, and eggs (gently), making sure the eggs are fully submerged, and bring to a rolling boil. Remove the eggs after 12 minutes and plunge them into an ice bath for 10 minutes. Continue to boil the potatoes and carrots until fork-tender, an additional 10–15 minutes. Drain and rinse with cold water.

Step 2. Peel and dice the eggs. Whisk all the ingredients for the lemon aioli together in a bowl.

Step 3. In a large bowl, mix together the potatoes, carrots, eggs, peas, pickles, and dill with the lemon aioli. Refrigerate for at least 6 hours or overnight. Serve chilled.

COOKING NOTES

This salad tastes best when chilled overnight. You can also serve it on a bed of greens.

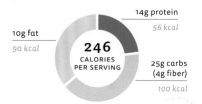

10g fat
90 kcal

14g protein
56 kcal

246
CALORIES
PER SERVING

25g carbs
(4g fiber)
100 kcal

SOUPS AND LENTILS

I must confess, sometimes I yearn for cooler weather so I can throw a bunch of ingredients in my Instant Pot and make an easy soup for dinner.

This chapter presents a selection of soups that are hearty, comforting, loaded with nutrients, and oh-so flavorful. Make soups in a rainbow of colors using a vegetable base such as tomato, cauliflower, spinach, or asparagus; keep them homely and hearty with a bean base such as the **Cuban Black Bean Soup** (page 112) or the Persian **Adasi** (page 123); or try a yogurt base, like my mom's **Cabbage Mor Kootu** (page 125) or the refreshing **Okroshka** (page 119), a cold summer soup.

Leftovers are often easily repurposed into pasta sauce or a dish like **Shakshuka** (page 133)! For a heartier meal, you can make wonderful pairings of these soups with a slice of **Zucchini Bread** (page 14), **Croutons** (page 109), or even a salad from the previous section.

1 Tbsp olive oil

2 small Indian green chiles, jalapeño peppers, or Thai chiles, slit lengthwise

2 Tbsp grated ginger

1 Tbsp minced garlic

3 cups/660ml water

1 medium head cauliflower (1 lb 5 oz/600g), leaves and stem trimmed, roughly chopped

¼ cup/28g raw cashews

¼ cup/30g yellow moong dal or split red lentils, soaked for 30 minutes, rinsed and drained

1 tsp salt

½ tsp ground turmeric

2 Tbsp lemon juice

1 Tbsp chopped cilantro/fresh coriander

½ tsp cracked black pepper

Loaded Cauliflower Soup

SERVES: 3

This was the first recipe I wrote down for this book. I converted my favorite dal to a soup with a creamy cauliflower base, a kick from the green chile, and a lift from ginger and lemon. This hearty soup is loaded with nutrients from the moong dal and cashews, a breeze to make, and just so delicious. I recommend serving with a slice of **Zucchini Bread** (page 14) or with **Croutons** (page 109). If you have leftovers, upcycle them into **Shakshuka** (page 133)!

Step 1. Heat the oil in a medium saucepan over medium heat. When hot, add the green chile, ginger, and garlic and sauté until fragrant, 1–2 minutes.

Step 2. Add the water, cauliflower, cashews, moong dal, salt, and turmeric and mix well.

Step 3. Bring to a boil. Reduce the heat, cover, and simmer until the lentils are fully cooked and the nuts are soft, 20–25 minutes. You can also pressure cook the mixture until done (15 minutes on high pressure, natural release in an Instant Pot).

Step 4. Blend the mixture until smooth with an immersion blender. Stir in the lemon juice, garnish with cilantro and black pepper, and serve.

COOKING NOTES

Freeze any leftovers in an airtight container for up to 3 months. Defrost in the microwave or at room temperature for 4–5 hours. You may need to pulse a couple of times with an immersion blender to fix the consistency after defrosting.

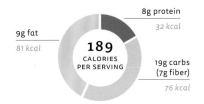

9g fat
81 kcal

8g protein
32 kcal

189
CALORIES
PER SERVING

19g carbs
(7g fiber)
76 kcal

8–9 plum or Roma tomatoes
(1 lb/450g), halved

2 small red bell peppers/capsicum
(9 oz/240g), roughly chopped

1 small onion (4 oz/110g), roughly
chopped

4–5 cloves garlic

1½ cups/360ml low-sodium
vegetable broth or water

1 tsp fine sea salt

½ tsp cracked black pepper

ZUCCHINI-BREAD
CROUTONS

1 Tbsp avocado oil, or other neutral
oil of choice

¼ tsp salt

¼ tsp cracked black pepper

¼ tsp garlic powder

¼ tsp dried oregano

1 slice Vegan Zucchini Bread
(2 oz/55g, *page 14*)

Roasted Red Pepper and Tomato Soup

SERVES: 2

This soup combines the best of summer produce, including tomatoes, red bell peppers, and zucchini. The croutons will quickly become a staple for both soups and salads. (I prefer to use the vegan zucchini bread to make croutons, as the original version tends to bring out an eggy flavor when roasted.)

This recipe began as a marinara recipe that I added broth to turn it into a soup. So when you need a pasta sauce, just skip the broth!

Step 1. Preheat the air fryer to 400°F/200°C or oven to 450°F/230°C.

Step 2. Place the tomatoes (skin-side down), peppers, onions, and garlic in the air fryer or on a foil-lined baking sheet. Spray lightly with oil. Air fry for 15 minutes, undisturbed, or bake for 30–40 minutes, turning over halfway through. The vegetables will be charred in spots. Leave the air fryer or oven on.

Step 3. Transfer the roasted vegetables to a medium saucepan, add the vegetable broth or water, salt, and pepper, and bring to a boil. Reduce the heat to low, cover, and simmer for 10–15 minutes.

Step 4. Meanwhile, to make the croutons, whisk together the oil, salt, pepper, garlic powder, and oregano in a bowl. Slice the zucchini bread into 1-x-¾ in/2.5-x-2cm pieces and mix together with the oil and spices. Air fry for 3–4 minutes, checking at 3 minutes, or bake for 8–10 minutes, turning halfway through and checking at 8 minutes, until dark golden brown and crisp.

Step 5. When the soup is done cooking, blend to your preferred consistency using an immersion blender. Divide the soup between two bowls, sprinkle with the croutons, and serve.

COOKING NOTES

Freeze any leftovers in an airtight container for up to 3 months. Defrost in the microwave, or at room temperature for 4–5 hours. You may need to pulse a couple of times with an immersion blender to fix the consistency after defrosting.

Freeze the croutons separately in an airtight bag for up to 6 months.

7g protein
28 kcal

12g fat
108 kcal

252
CALORIES
PER SERVING

29g carbs
(8g fiber)
116 kcal

LENTIL FILLING

2 Tbsp olive oil

1 medium onion (7 oz/200g), diced

1 medium green bell pepper/
capsicum (7 oz/200g), diced

2 Tbsp tomato paste

1 Tbsp minced garlic

1 Tbsp cornstarch/cornflour

2 tsp fine sea salt

2 tsp dried oregano

½ tsp red chile flakes

1 cup/120g dried green or brown
lentils

4 cups/960ml low-sodium vegetable
broth, divided

2 cups/320g frozen green peas,
defrosted

CAULI MASH

1 ½ lb/680g cauliflower or
cauliflower rice

2 oz/56g butter

1½ tsp cracked black pepper

½ tsp salt

1 cup/112g grated Parmesan cheese

TO VEGANIZE
For the cauli mash, use
olive oil in place of the
butter and nutritional yeast
in place of the Parmesan.

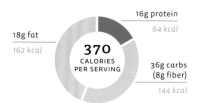

18g fat
162 kcal

16g protein
64 kcal

370
CALORIES
PER SERVING

36g carbs
(8g fiber)
144 kcal

Shepherd's Pie

SERVES: 6

Shepherd's pie is a classic British dish, usually made from ground meat with a mashed potato topping. A colleague brought a root vegetable version to a Thanksgiving potluck at my office and I was hooked! In my recipe, I use lentils for a higher-protein filling, and a creamy cauli mash that will be gone in a jiffy.

Step 1. For the lentil filling, heat a medium saucepan over medium-high heat. When hot, add the olive oil and onions and cook, stirring often, until the onions are light brown and caramelized, about 5 minutes. Add the bell pepper and cook for 2 minutes. Reduce the heat to medium. Add the tomato paste, garlic, cornstarch, salt, oregano, and chile flakes, mix well, and cook for 1 minute.

Step 2. Add the lentils and 3 cups of broth, mix well, and bring to a boil. Simmer, adding up to 1 cup of additional broth as needed, until the lentils are fully cooked, 20–25 minutes. Add the peas toward the end and cook until the mixture is very thick. Turn off the stove.

Step 3. While the lentils are cooking, preheat the oven to 350°F/180°C and grease an 8-x-8-x-1½ in/20-x-20-x-4-cm pan.

Step 4. To make the cauliflower mash, bring a pot of salted water to a boil and cook the cauliflower until tender, 6–8 minutes. Drain. Heat the butter in a small saucepan over medium heat. When the butter melts, add the garlic, salt, and pepper and cook until fragrant, about 1 minute. Combine the cauliflower, butter-garlic mixture, and Parmesan in a food processor and puree until smooth. Taste and add more salt and pepper as needed.

Step 5. To assemble the pie, spoon the lentils into the prepared pan and tap lightly on the counter to settle. Add the cauliflower mash on top and smooth into an even layer with a spatula or butter knife.

Step 6. Bake for 25–30 minutes, or until the top is browned in spots. You can also broil the pie for 1 minute to brown it faster, if desired. Serve hot.

COOKING NOTES

Prepare 1 day ahead and refrigerate; it becomes easier to slice and serve.

Freeze leftovers in an airtight container for up to 2 months. Defrost in the microwave, or leave out for 4–5 hours at room temperature.

2 Tbsp olive oil

1½ cups diced onion (5 oz/150g)

2 bay leaves

1½ cups diced green bell pepper/
capsicum (5 oz/150g)

1 small jalapeño pepper, diced and
seeded to adjust spice level to taste

1 small plum or Roma tomato
(2 oz/60g), diced

2 Tbsp minced garlic

2 tsp ground cumin

2 tsp dried oregano

2 tsp smoked paprika

1 ½ tsp salt

1 heaping cup/200g dried black
beans or 2 (15-oz/400-g) cans,
drained and rinsed (see cooking note)

2 ½ cups/600ml water

1 avocado (7 oz/200g), sliced,
for garnish

3 Tbsp chopped cilantro/fresh
coriander, for garnish

Cuban Black Bean Soup

SERVES: 4

This Latin-American take on beans is generously spiced and
typically served with rice. With a few easy modifications, I've
converted it into a hearty soup that's topped off with avocado to cool
it down just a tad. Leftovers make a wonderful topping for **Huevos
Rancheros** (page 134)!

Step 1. Heat a medium sauté pan over medium heat. If you are
planning to cook beans on the stove, use a medium saucepan for
which you have a lid.

Step 2. When the sauté pan is hot, add the olive oil, onion, and bay
leaves and cook, stirring, until the onion is soft, about 5 minutes.

Step 3. Add the bell pepper and jalapeño, increase the heat to
medium-high, and cook for 1–2 minutes.

Step 4. Add the tomato, garlic, cumin, oregano, paprika, and salt,
reduce the heat to medium, and cook, stirring, until the tomatoes
break down and start oozing, and the spices are fragrant, 3–4 minutes.
Add 2–3 tablespoons of water to deglaze the pan if needed.

Step 5. If using a pressure cooker, transfer the sautéed vegetables
to the cooker and add the black beans and 2½ cups/600ml water
for dried beans or 2 cups/480 ml water if using canned beans. If
cooking on the stove, add the canned beans and 2 cups/480 ml
water to the saucepan (see cooking note).

Step 6. Pressure cook until done (40 minutes on high pressure in an
Instant Pot, or 20 minutes if using canned beans, natural release). If
cooking on the stovetop, bring to a boil and simmer, covered, until
cooked, about 40 minutes for canned beans.

Step 7. Remove the bay leaves, add more water if desired, and pulse
a few times with an immersion blender for a soup that still has
some texture. Garnish with avocado slices and cilantro and serve.

COOKING NOTES

If you don't have a pressure cooker, I would recommend using
canned beans.

Freeze any leftovers in an airtight container for up to 3 months.
Defrost in the microwave, or at room temperature for 4–5 hours.

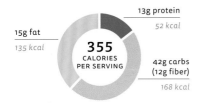

15g fat
135 kcal

13g protein
52 kcal

355
CALORIES
PER SERVING

42g carbs
(12g fiber)
168 kcal

1 Tbsp olive oil

1 medium onion (7 oz/200g), diced

1 bay leaf

1 Tbsp minced garlic

2 cups/480ml water

12–15 spears asparagus (1 lb/450g), trimmed and halved

1 tsp salt

1 tsp ground cumin

½ tsp garam masala

2 Tbsp dry shredded coconut (unsweetened), for garnish

½ tsp cracked black pepper, for garnish

Pinch of red chile flakes, for garnish

Curried Asparagus Soup

SERVES: 2

This delicate soup is perfect for spring when asparagus is in season! I give it a mild curry flavor and then garnish with crispy coconut for extra texture. It goes wonderfully well with a slice of **Zucchini Bread** (page 14) or a side salad.

Step 1. Heat a medium saucepan over medium-high heat. Once hot, add the olive oil and onions and cook, stirring often, until the onions are lightly browned, about 5 minutes. Add the bay leaf and garlic and cook for 1 minute.

Step 2. Add the water, asparagus, salt, cumin, and garam masala and mix well.

Step 3. Bring to a boil, then simmer, covered, until the asparagus is tender, 20–30 minutes.

Step 4. Remove the bay leaf and blend the soup until smooth with an immersion blender. Taste and add more salt as needed. Garnish with coconut, black pepper, and chile flakes and serve.

COOKING NOTES

You can dry-roast the coconut on the stovetop, if desired: Cook in a frying pan over medium-low heat, stirring often, for 5–10 minutes, until golden brown.

Freeze any leftovers in an airtight container for up to 3 months. You may need to pulse a couple of times with a blender to fix the consistency after defrosting.

11g fat
99 kcal

6g protein
24 kcal

199
CALORIES
PER SERVING

19g carbs
(8g fiber)
76 kcal

1 Tbsp olive oil

1 small onion (4 oz/110g), roughly chopped

1 large clove garlic, minced

3 cups low-sodium vegetable broth or water

1 tsp. ground cumin

1 tsp salt

½ tsp cracked black pepper

¼ tsp red chile flakes

1 cup/160g frozen green peas

1 lb/450g fresh spinach

1 Tbsp lemon juice

3 oz/84g paneer (defrosted if frozen), cubed

Spring Pea and Spinach Soup

SERVES: 3

This soup is just wholesome goodness; so much so that I crave it when I'm sick. I start with a gorgeous green saag-esque broth using spinach, and then add sweet peas for a thicker consistency. The flavor is deliberately kept delicate, but you can add a teaspoon of garam masala if you like. Garnishing with fresh paneer makes it filling and adds extra protein.

Step 1. Heat a deep saucepan over medium-high. Add the olive oil and onion and cook, stirring often, until the onions are lightly brown, about 5 minutes. Add the garlic and cook for 30 seconds or until aromatic.

Step 2. Add the broth, cumin, salt, pepper, and chile flakes and bring to a boil.

Step 3. Add the peas and cook until soft, 2–3 minutes.

Step 4. Add the spinach gradually and cook until bright green and wilted.

Step 5. Turn off the stove and blend the mixture until smooth with an immersion blender. Stir in the lemon juice.

Step 6. If the paneer is cold from the fridge, warm it for 2 minutes in hot water to make it soft. Garnish the soup with the paneer cubes and serve.

COOKING NOTES

Leftovers freeze well and are also great upcycled into **Shakshuka** (page 133)! You may need to pulse a couple of times with a blender to fix the consistency after defrosting (remove the paneer before you blend).

12g fat
108 kcal

240 CALORIES PER SERVING

13g protein
52 kcal

20g carbs (6g fiber)
80 kcal

1½ cups/200g peeled and diced jicama or radish

2 eggs

2 large red radishes (1 oz/30g), sliced into wedges

1 small, unpeeled cucumber (7 oz/200g), diced

2 medium scallions (1 oz/30g), chopped

1 Tbsp chopped fresh dill

¼ tsp fine sea salt

¼ tsp cracked black pepper

2 cups/480ml whole-milk kefir or buttermilk (or diluted yogurt)

½ cup/120ml water, as needed

Okroshka

SERVES: 2

When it's too hot to turn on your oven, you make okroshka! The friendly owner of a lovely little café in Prague made it for us when she learned we were vegetarian. This refreshing but hearty Russian cold soup is usually made with kvass, a sparkling fermented beverage, but you can also use kefir or yogurt. I substitute jicama for the potato in this recipe to make it lowish-carb. It is so pretty, with pink radish and dill floating to the surface, and somehow manages to satisfy both thirst and hunger on a summer afternoon.

Step 1. Bring a pot of salted water to a boil. Add the jicama and cook until soft, 20–30 minutes (see cooking note). Drain and rinse with cold water.

Step 2. Meanwhile, hard-boil the eggs. Place the eggs in a medium saucepan, add enough water to submerge them, and bring to a rolling boil. Boil for 10–12 minutes. Turn off the stove, cover, and let sit for 10 minutes. Plunge the eggs into an ice bath, peel, and dice.

Step 3. Divide the jicama, eggs, radishes, cucumber, scallions, dill, salt, and pepper between two bowls. Add ¼ cup/60ml of water to the kefir and mix well. Add more water if desired. Pour the diluted kefir over the ingredients in the two bowls and mix.

Step 4. Season with additional salt and pepper to taste. Chill for 3–4 hours before serving.

COOKING NOTES

If you are using radish instead of the jicama, you will need less time to cook in Step 1, about 10 minutes, and you can boil it along with the eggs.

16g protein
64 kcal

13g fat
117 kcal

289
CALORIES
PER SERVING

27g carbs
(9g fiber)
108 kcal

2 Tbsp butter

2 heaping cups thinly sliced yellow onion (12 oz/340g)

¼ cup/60ml dry white wine or water, for deglazing

1 Tbsp minced garlic

1 Tbsp cornstarch/cornflour

1 Tbsp water

3 cups/720ml low-sodium vegetable broth or water

1 tsp vegan Worcestershire sauce

1 bay leaf

¼ tsp dried oregano

¼ tsp dried thyme, or 1 sprig fresh thyme

¼ tsp fine sea salt

¼ tsp cracked black pepper

2 slices **Zucchini Bread** (*page 14*; 2 oz/55g each)

½ cup/56g sharp grated Cheddar cheese (or Gruyère, which is traditional but usually not vegetarian)

> **TO VEGANIZE**
> Use olive oil in place of butter and **Vegan Zucchini Bread** (page 14). Use vegan cheese or skip the cheese.

French Onion Soup

SERVES: 2

I've always wondered why it's so hard to find vegetarian French onion soup in restaurants, given that caramelized onions are the star of the soup. It was a no-brainer to include my version in this book, particularly when I get another chance to showcase my zucchini bread. This is an easy and craveable soup that will leave your kitchen smelling amazing.

Step 1. Heat a medium saucepan over medium heat. When hot, add the butter and onions and cook, stirring often, until the onions turn a deep brown and the liquid evaporates. As the onions cook, add a splash of wine as needed to deglaze the bottom and scrape up bits sticking to the bottom of the pan. The whole process should take 15–20 minutes.

Step 2. Turn the heat down to medium, add the garlic, and cook for 1 minute. Stir the cornstarch and water together in a small bowl to make a slurry. Add the slurry to the saucepan and mix well.

Step 3. Add the broth, Worcestershire sauce, bay leaf, oregano, thyme, salt, and pepper and bring to a boil. Reduce the heat to medium-low and simmer until the broth is rich and slightly thickened, 20–30 minutes. Remove the bay leaf.

Step 4. While the broth is simmering, preheat the oven to 400°F/200°C.

Step 5. Lightly spray the bread with oil and bake on a parchment-lined baking sheet for 3–4 minutes, or until lightly browned on both sides.

Step 6. Remove the baking sheet from the oven, sprinkle the cheese on the bread, and preheat the broiler. Broil the bread until the cheese melts, 1–2 minutes. Portion the soup into bowls, top each bowl with a piece of toast, and serve.

COOKING NOTES

If you have oven-safe soup bowls or crocks, you can place them on the baking sheet in Step 6, fill with soup, place the bread with cheese on top of each bowl, and broil them directly.

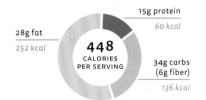

15g protein
60 kcal

28g fat
252 kcal

448
CALORIES
PER SERVING

34g carbs
(6g fiber)
136 kcal

2 Tbsp olive oil

1 small onion (4 oz/110g), diced

1 bay leaf

1 Tbsp minced garlic

1 tsp ground cumin

1 tsp fine sea salt

½ tsp cracked black pepper

¼ tsp ground turmeric

½ cup/100g diced radish

½ heaping cup/75g dried green or brown lentils

2 cups low-sodium vegetable broth or water

1 Tbsp lemon juice

1 Tbsp chopped fresh Italian parsley

Adasi

SERVES: 2

In my early days in New York City, I had a lovely dinner at Café Nadery (sadly closed now), which served homestyle Persian food in the West Village. One of my takeaways from that meal was this lentil soup called adasi. Often served for breakfast in Iran, it also makes an easy, delicious, and comforting one-pot dinner on chilly nights. I replace the traditional potato with radish to make this soup lower in carbs, but you can also just leave it out or add any other vegetables of your choice.

Step 1. Heat a medium saucepan over medium-high heat. When hot, add the olive oil, onion, and bay leaf and cook, stirring often, until the onions are golden brown, about 5 minutes.

Step 2. Add the garlic, cumin, salt, pepper, and turmeric, mix well, and cook until fragrant, about 1 minute.

Step 3. Add the radish, lentils, and stock and bring to a boil. Cover, reduce the heat, and simmer for 20–30 minutes, until the lentils are well cooked.

Step 4. Season with additional salt and pepper to taste. Turn off the stove and mix in the lemon juice. Garnish with parsley and serve.

10g protein
40 kcal

15g fat
135 kcal

307
CALORIES
PER SERVING

33g carbs
(6g fiber)
132 kcal

1½ cups/360ml water

½ tsp salt

½ head green cabbage (12 oz/350g), shredded or finely diced

½ tsp ground turmeric

MASALA PASTE

1–2 Indian green chiles, jalapeño peppers, or Thai chiles, depending on desired heat level

2 Tbsp fresh or frozen shredded coconut or unsweetened dry shredded coconut

1 Tbsp chana dal (split chickpeas), soaked for 30 minutes and drained

1 tsp coriander seeds or ¾ tsp ground coriander seed

1 tsp cumin seeds

1 cup/220g whole-milk plain Greek yogurt

TADKA (TEMPERING)

2 tsp avocado oil, or other neutral oil of choice

1 tsp black mustard seeds

½ tsp urad dal (black gram, split and skinned)

¼ tsp asafoetida (hing, sometimes called yellow powder)

TO VEGANIZE
Use vegan yogurt in place of the whole-milk Greek yogurt.

Cabbage Mor Kootu

SERVES: 2

A spiced yogurt stew is a common main served alongside steamed rice in South Indian homes. Often it will include white pumpkin or chayote and other vegetables. This version with cabbage is my mom's specialty and is basically soul food for me. I categorize this recipe as a soup in this book, but you can also serve it over cooked cauliflower rice.

Step 1. In a medium saucepan, add the water and salt and bring to a boil. Add the cabbage, turmeric, and salt, mix, and cook until the cabbage is tender, 20–30 minutes. Drain, saving 1 cup/240ml of the cabbage water to use later.

Step 2. To make the masala paste, combine all the ingredients in a small food processor and blend to a coarse mixture (the texture of sand), adding 1–2 tablespoons of the cabbage water as needed.

Step 3. In a bowl, whisk the yogurt with ½ cup/120ml of the cabbage water until smooth. Set aside.

Step 4. To make the tadka, rinse the same saucepan used to boil the cabbage and place over medium-high heat. When hot, add the oil and mustard seeds. When the mustard seeds pop, reduce the heat to medium and add the urad dal and the asafoetida.

Step 5. When urad dal turns golden brown, add the cooked cabbage and masala paste, mix well, and cook for 2–3 minutes. Add the diluted yogurt, mix well, and cook until heated throughout (do not boil), 2–3 minutes. Add more cabbage water if desired.

Step 6. Season with salt and serve hot.

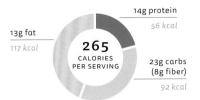

14g protein
56 kcal

13g fat
117 kcal

265
CALORIES
PER SERVING

23g carbs
(8g fiber)
92 kcal

EGGS

Brunch is often synonymous with egg-based dishes—easy, filling, nutritious, and perfect for when you need to rustle up a meal quickly. Forget the usual omelette or scramble; in this chapter I turn the spotlight on three traditional egg preparations from around the world: **Okonomiyaki** (page 129) from Japan, **Shakshuka** (page 133) from the Middle East, and **Huevos Rancheros** (page 134) from Mexico. I also have a little fun with **Eggs Florentine** (page 137) and a somewhat unique adaptation of the Indian **Kathi Roll** (page 130). Happy brunching!

GREEK YOGURT MAYO

¼ cup/55g whole-milk plain Greek yogurt

1 tsp rice vinegar or white or apple cider vinegar

1 tsp Dijon mustard

¼ tsp salt

¼ tsp cracked black pepper

PANCAKES

½ cup/56g blanched almond flour

¼ tsp baking powder

½ tsp salt

¼ cup/60ml water

2 eggs

2 heaping cups/200g finely shredded green cabbage

4 medium scallions (2 oz/55g), chopped and divided into white and green parts

2 tsp olive oil, divided

1 Tbsp vegan Worcestershire sauce or any BBQ sauce

TOPPINGS

Red or white pickled ginger

Nori (seaweed flakes)

White sesame seeds

25g fat
225 kcal

361
CALORIES
PER SERVING

17g protein
68 kcal

17g carbs
(6g fiber)
68 kcal

Okonomiyaki

SERVES: 2

In Tokyo, my husband and I went to a traditional teppanyaki restaurant, where one of my husband's kind colleagues convinced the staff to make us a vegetarian okonomiyaki. They did this on a large griddle right in front of us, cooking a hearty pancake with eggs, flour, and a surprising amount of shredded cabbage folded in. "Okonomiyaki" means "grilled as you like it," and can be served with a variety of toppings. In my version, I use almond flour, vegan Worcestershire sauce, and a Greek yogurt–based mayo.

Step 1. Combine all the ingredients for the Greek yogurt mayo and pulse a couple of times in a blender until smooth.

Step 2. Combine the almond flour, baking powder, and salt in a bowl. Add the water and mix well. Heat a medium nonstick pan over medium heat and lightly spray with oil.

Step 3. Spoon half the batter into a bowl. Beat one egg in a small bowl and add it to the batter. Add half the cabbage, half the white parts of the scallions, and 1 teaspoon of oil. Mix well with a spoon and pour onto the pan to make a pancake about 6 in/15cm wide and ⅓ in/1cm thick. Pat the mixture gently with the back of the spoon or a measuring cup to flatten. Cook until brown on the bottom, 3–4 minutes, then gently release the bottom and carefully flip (see cooking note). Cook on the other side until done, 2–3 minutes, and transfer to a plate.

Step 4. Repeat to prepare the second pancake with the remaining batter. Brush each pancake with Worcestershire sauce. Drizzle the mayo in a zig-zag motion on top—I use a squeeze bottle to do this, but you can also use a spoon; the goal is just to get it on the pancake.

Step 5. Sprinkle each pancake with toppings as desired and serve.

COOKING NOTES

Flipping can be tricky. If you don't have a wide omelette spatula, use a plate to slide the pancake from the pan and then flip the plate over the pan in a quick motion. Don't worry if it breaks, just push it back together with the spatula. It's all going to be covered anyway!

SHAWARMA SPICE BLEND

2 tsp garam masala

1½ tsp ground cumin

1 tsp paprika

1 tsp ground turmeric

¾ tsp smoked paprika

¾ tsp ground coriander seed

¼ tsp salt

1 Tbsp + 2 tsp olive oil, divided

1 tsp grated ginger

1 tsp minced garlic

1 lb/450g small cauliflower florets (1½ in/1¼-cm pieces)

2–3 Tbsp water, as needed

RAITA

¼ cup/55g whole-milk plain Greek yogurt

1 baby cucumber or ⅓ large cucumber (3½ oz/100g)

¼ tsp. salt

¼ tsp. cracked black pepper

4 eggs

1/2 tsp salt, divided

1/2 tsp cracked black pepper, divided

TO VEGANIZE

Use vegan yogurt for the raita and a **Chickpea Crepe** (page 18) in place of the omelette.

24g fat
216 kcal

20g protein
80 kcal

356 CALORIES PER SERVING

15g carbs (5g fiber)
60 kcal

Unda Kathi Roll

SERVES: 2

Funnily enough, I never ate a kathi roll when I lived in India. The first time I tried one was actually in New York, at the Kati Roll Company in the West Village! It is a rather clever concept: wrap the sabzi in the roti and get it all in one delicious bite. This recipe uses an omelette ("unda" means "egg") to make a high-protein wrap, which is stuffed with the most decadent cauliflower shawarma and raita.

Step 1. Mix all the ingredients for the shawarma spice blend in a large bowl.

Step 2. Add 1 tablespoon of oil, the ginger, and garlic to the spice blend and mix well to make a marinade. Add the cauliflower florets and toss until they are well coated with the marinade.

Step 3. Heat a medium sauté pan over medium heat. Add the cauliflower florets and 2 tablespoons water and mix. Cover and cook, stirring occasionally and adding another tablespoon of water to deglaze the pan if needed, until the florets are soft and a deep golden brown, 15–20 minutes.

Step 4. Mix all the ingredients for the raita and set aside.

Step 5. To make each wrap, beat 2 eggs together with ¼ teaspoon each salt and pepper in a bowl. Heat a medium nonstick frying pan over medium heat. Add 1 teaspoon of oil and swirl the pan to coat the sides. Pour the eggs into the pan, swirl the pan to coat the bottom fully, and cook, pushing the dry edges gently toward the center with the spatula so the liquid egg from the center flows to the sides, until the top is just cooked, 3–4 minutes. Carefully transfer to a plate and repeat for the second omelette.

Step 6. To assemble, spoon half the raita into the center of each omelette and add the cauliflower. Fold the sides to make a wrap. Use a 12 x 6 in/30 x 15cm sheet of foil to wrap the bottom half of each kathi roll to hold it together. Serve hot.

2½ cups/600ml soup of choice

4 eggs

¼ tsp fine sea salt, for garnish

½ tsp cracked black pepper,
for garnish

¼ tsp chile flakes, for garnish

1 Tbsp chopped fresh parsley,
for garnish

Shakshuka

SERVES: 2

Traditionally, shakshuka is eggs poached in a tomato-onion sauce, but this is also a delicious way to "upcycle" any soup leftovers. The rainbow of shakshukas in the picture features my **Roasted Red Pepper and Tomato Soup** (page 109), **Spring Pea and Spinach Soup** (page 116), and **Loaded Cauliflower Soup** (page 106). If you'd like, add a slice of **Zucchini Bread** (page 14) for dipping.

Step 1. Heat the soup in a large oven-safe skillet over medium heat. Preheat the oven to 375°F/190°C.

Step 2. When the soup is just starting to boil, make a well near the perimeter and carefully crack an egg into it. Spoon some of the soup over the egg whites to hold the egg in place. Repeat for the remaining eggs.

Step 3. Carefully transfer the skillet to the oven and bake for 8–10 minutes, until the whites are set but the yolks still jiggle. The eggs will continue to cook in the residual heat.

Step 4. Sprinkle with salt, pepper, chile flakes, and parsley and serve.

COOKING NOTES

You can also continue to cook on the stove with a lid on for 8–10 minutes in Step 3, instead of using the oven.

If making a larger batch, heat the soup separately on the stove or in the microwave and then transfer to a baking pan or casserole dish. Bake at 375°F/190°C as in Step 3.

20g fat
180 kcal

344
CALORIES
PER SERVING

21g protein
84 kcal

20g carbs
(7g fiber)
80 kcal

* Nutrition per serving (with **Loaded Cauliflower Soup**; nutrition facts will vary depending on soup used)

1 recipe **Chickpea Crepe** batter
(page 18), prepared through Step 1

SPICY TOMATO SALSA

2 medium plum or Roma tomatoes
(½ lb/225g)

2 heaping Tbsp diced onion

2 Tbsp chopped cilantro/fresh
coriander

1 small jalapeño pepper, or Indian
green chile, or Thai chile, seeded to
adjust to your desired spice level

1 large clove garlic

1 Tbsp lime juice

½ Tbsp balsamic vinegar

¼ tsp salt

¼ tsp cracked black pepper

¼ tsp ground cumin

Pinch of dried oregano

4 tsp olive oil, divided

½ heaping cup/100g dried black
beans, pressure cooked until done,
or 1 (15-oz/400-g) can, drained and
rinsed

4 eggs

1 medium avocado (7 oz/200g),
scooped and sliced

1 oz/28g cotija cheese or feta,
crumbled

Huevos Rancheros

SERVES: 4

Huevos Rancheros or ranch-style eggs is one of my favorite brunch
dishes because it has so much more than eggs! You will love my
chickpea crepe that gets fried to make a crispy tortilla, then layered
with black beans, a fried egg, and a fiery tomato salsa that I've
tinkered with for years. It is finished off with avocado and cotija
cheese for a result that will leave you licking your lips.

Step 1. As the crepe batter rests, make the salsa. Pulse all the
ingredients together in a food processor or blender to your desired
level of chunkiness. Refrigerate until ready to use.

Step 2. Heat a lightly greased small nonstick frying pan over medium
heat. When hot, add 1 teaspoon of oil and swirl the pan gently to coat
the sides. Stir the crepe batter and pour ¼ cup/60ml of batter into
the pan; it should sizzle as it hits the pan. Swirl the pan to coat the
sides and cook until you see the crepe dry completely, 1–2 minutes.
Use a spatula to peek at the bottom; it should be a nice golden brown.
Flip carefully and cook the other side until crisp, about 1 minute.
Transfer to a plate and repeat with the remaining oil and batter to
make 3 more crepes.

Step 3. If desired, warm up the black beans in the microwave or on
the stove. Mash lightly with the back of a spoon and layer them on
each crepe.

Step 4. Heat the same nonstick frying pan over medium-low and
use an oil spray to lightly grease. Fry the eggs sunny-side up. Place
an egg on top of the black beans on each crepe.

Step 5. Spoon some of the salsa over each crepe, and top with
avocado slices. Garnish with cotija cheese and serve.

COOKING NOTES

You may find that the first crepe is a little hard to get off the pan—
just let it cook longer until it is easy to flip. The pan will be the right
temperature and seasoned well for the second crepe.

If you have leftovers from the **Cuban Black Bean Soup** (page 112),
you can use those instead of the black beans!

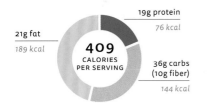

21g fat
189 kcal

19g protein
76 kcal

409
CALORIES
PER SERVING

36g carbs
(10g fiber)
144 kcal

1½ tsp olive oil

2 tsp minced garlic

12 oz/340g fresh spinach, defrosted if frozen

¾ tsp fine sea salt, divided

¼ tsp red chile flakes

4 slices **Zucchini Bread** (page 14), approximately 2 oz/55g each

4 thick slices of tomato (6 oz/170g)

4 eggs

½ tsp cracked black pepper, for garnish

Eggs Florentine

SERVES: 2

I wasn't sure if I should include a pedestrian item such as poached eggs on bread in this book, but the opportunity to highlight my zucchini bread won again. My version of this quintessential brunch dish keeps it simple—poached eggs on a layer of chile-garlic spinach and a thick slice of tomato. When the yolk oozes onto the bread, it makes all the sauce you'll ever need. (But I won't mind if you drizzle your favorite hot sauce over the egg before serving.)

Step 1. Heat the oil in a medium sauté pan over medium heat. Add the garlic and sauté until fragrant, a few seconds. Add the spinach gradually and cook until just wilted. Add ½ teaspoon salt and the chile flakes, mix well, and cook until incorporated, 1–2 minutes.

Step 2. Lightly spray each slice of bread with oil and toast on both sides. Place on 2 plates and layer each with the spinach and a slice of tomato.

Step 3. To poach the eggs (see cooking note), bring a large saucepan filled two-thirds full with water to a boil and then reduce the heat to a gentle simmer. Crack the eggs carefully into individual cups, keeping the yolks intact. Gently tip the eggs into the saucepan one by one. Cook for 3 minutes and remove with a slotted spoon.

Step 4. Add a poached egg on top of each slice of toast. Garnish with the remaining ¼ teaspoon of salt and the pepper and serve.

COOKING NOTES

Here's a nifty way to soft-boil whole eggs, in their shells, in the Instant Pot. Pour a cup of water into the inner pot. Arrange eggs on a trivet and place inside the inner pot. cook on high pressure for 4 minutes, quick release the pressure, and dunk in an ice bath for 2 minutes before peeling.

30g protein
120 kcal

28g fat
252 kcal

492
CALORIES
PER SERVING

30g carbs
(11g fiber)
120 kcal

SMALL PLATES

This section includes a wide variety of party-ready recipes, from lighthearted, popular favorites like **Masala Egg Bites** (page 141), **Zucchini Chips** (page 156), and **(Over)Stuffed Mini Peppers** (page 148) to little bites inspired by the world's cuisines, such as the **Mezze Platter** (page 142) of the Middle East, the **Empanadas with Chimichurri** (page 146) of Latin America, and the **Masala Vada** (page 152) of South India. I hope you find some favorites here that you can pass around at happy hour, wow guests with at a dinner party, or just use for a filling snack.

4 eggs

½ cup/113g full-fat cottage cheese

½ cup/56g shredded Cheddar cheese

½ cup/75g diced red bell pepper/
capsicum

2 Tbsp diced onion

2 Tbsp chopped cilantro/fresh
coriander

1 Indian green chile, jalapeño pepper,
or Thai chile, chopped

1 tsp grated ginger

½ tsp ground turmeric

¼ tsp salt

Masala Egg Bites

SERVES: 6   *makes 24*

These fluffy mini frittatas or egg muffins are spiced with a simple combination of ginger, green chile, and turmeric to take the ubiquitous coffee-chain egg bites up a notch. They are great for meal prep, make a fast but filling breakfast or snack on the go, and clock in at approximately 25 calories per bite. You can mix up the toppings as you like—feel free to use spinach, roasted red pepper, goat cheese, or any other veggies or cheeses you like.

Step 1. Preheat the oven to 350°F/175°C. Lightly grease a 24-cup mini muffin pan with nonstick spray. (If using a regular muffin pan, increase the baking time by 5 minutes in Step 5.)

Step 2. Combine the eggs, cottage cheese, and Cheddar cheese in a blender or food processor and blend until smooth. The mixture will be the consistency of heavy cream/double cream.

Step 3. Add all the other ingredients to the blender and pulse a couple of times until evenly distributed (we don't want to blend the toppings smooth, just distribute them evenly throughout the mixture).

Step 4. Pour the mixture into the prepared mini muffin pan, filling each muffin cup no more than two-thirds full.

Step 5. Bake for 15 minutes, or until golden brown on top. Let cool in the pan (they will deflate a bit). Remove from the pan and serve.

COOKING NOTES

Store in an airtight container in the refrigerator for up to 4 days. Reheat for 20 seconds in the microwave. They are also freezer friendly—just wrap them individually in plastic wrap to prevent them from sticking together, and freeze for up to 1 month.

9g protein
36 kcal

7g fat
63 kcal

107
CALORIES
PER SERVING

2g carbs
(0g fiber)
8 kcal

1 cup/120g chickpea flour

1 cup/240ml warm water, divided

2 Tbsp olive oil

1 tsp minced garlic

1 tsp ground cumin

½ tsp salt

1 tsp baking powder

1 tsp za'atar seasoning, for garnish (optional)

1 tsp sesame seeds, for garnish (optional)

HUMMUS

½ heaping cup/100g dried chickpeas, soaked overnight with a pinch of baking soda, or 1 (15-oz/400-g) can chickpeas

3 Tbsp lemon juice

2 Tbsp olive oil

1 small clove garlic, minced

1 Tbsp white sesame seeds

1 tsp ground cumin

1 tsp paprika

½ tsp cracked black pepper

½ tsp fine sea salt

(continued opposite)

Mezze Platter

SERVES: 8

I dream ardently about doing a food tour of the Middle East someday, where the food always feels like home. Until then, here's a mezze platter that fills my heart.

Muhammara is a tangy red pepper-walnut chutney that originated in the Syrian city of Aleppo, while tzatziki is a thicker yogurt dip that resembles the Indian raita. Hummus, of course, needs no introduction. The traditional preparation for hummus is to make tahini first, but I like to throw in the sesame seeds along with everything else to keep things simple. Any added texture is a bonus! My fluffy chickpea "pita" will quickly become a favorite, not just for this platter but also as a substitute for naan to mop up curries.

Step 1. To make the pita batter, place the chickpea flour in a bowl, add ½ cup/120ml of warm water, and mix until smooth. Add the remaining ½ cup/120ml water and stir. Heat the olive oil in a small frying pan over medium heat. Add the garlic, cumin, and salt and cook, stirring, until fragrant, about 1 minute. Add the oil-spice mixture to the batter and stir until incorporated. Rest the batter for 30 minutes to 1 hour at room temperature.

Step 2. To make the pitas, heat the same pan over medium-high heat. Add the baking powder to the batter and stir (this makes the pitas fluffy like a pancake!). Pour about ¼ cup/60ml of batter into the pan and cook until almost dry on top, 1–2 minutes. Sprinkle with ⅛ teaspoon each sesame seeds and za'atar seasoning, if using. When dry, flip carefully and cook on the other side for 1 minute. Transfer to a plate. Repeat to make 7 more pitas, lightly spraying the pan with the oil between batches if necessary.

Step 3. To make the hummus, if using dried chickpeas, drain and rinse the soaked chickpeas. Pressure cook the chickpeas along with 1½ cups/360ml of water until done (30 minutes at high pressure, natural release in an Instant Pot). Drain, reserving ½ cup/120ml of the chickpea liquid. If using canned chickpeas, drain and reserve the liquid for the next step.

Step 4. Combine the chickpeas, 2 tablespoons of the chickpea liquid, and all the remaining ingredients in a blender or food

18g fat
162 kcal

10g protein
40 kcal

294
CALORIES
PER SERVING

23g carbs
(5g fiber)
92 kcal

MUHAMMARA

1 medium red bell pepper/capsicum
(7 oz/200g; *see cooking notes*)

½ cup/56g toasted walnuts

2 Tbsp breadcrumbs from **Vegan Zucchini Bread** (page 14; *see cooking notes*)

1 small clove garlic

1–2 Tbsp lemon juice, to taste

1 Tbsp olive oil

1 Tbsp pomegranate molasses, or
1 Tbsp lime juice + a dash of honey

1 Tbsp Aleppo chile flakes, or 2 tsp sweet paprika + ½ tsp cayenne

½ tsp ground cumin

¼ tsp fine sea salt

TZATZIKI (PAGE 44)

processor and blend until smooth, adding additional chickpea liquid or water, 1 tablespoon at a time, as needed to achieve the desired consistency.

Step 5. To make the muhammara, slice the bell pepper into 5–6 large strips. Preheat the air fryer to 360°F/180°C or oven to 400°F/200°C. Lightly spray the air fryer base or a baking sheet with oil. Add the pepper strips and air fry for 10 minutes, turning halfway through, or bake for 15–20 minutes, turning halfway through. The peppers should be shrunken and charred in spots with the skin peeling off. Reduce the oven temperature or preheat the oven to 300°F/150°C.

Step 6. Combine the peppers and all the remaining ingredients together in the food processor and blend, adding a little water if needed to reach the desired consistency.

Step 7. Prepare the tzatziki according to the directions on page 44.

Step 8. To serve, cut the pita into triangles and serve with the dips.

COOKING NOTES

Hummus and muhammara can be prepared up to 3 days in advance and refrigerated. Freeze in an airtight container for up to 3 months and defrost by leaving out at room temperature for 4–5 hours or overnight.

For the muhammara, you can save time by using 1½ cups/200g store-bought roasted red peppers and 2 Tbsp. store-bought panko breadcrumbs, if you wish, rather than making your own.

Mezze Platter,
page 142

Empanadas with Chimichurri,
page 146

EMPANADA DOUGH

1 cup/120g chickpea flour

½ tsp salt

2 oz/56g cold butter

2 tsp white vinegar

1 egg, lightly beaten

1 Tbsp cornstarch/cornflour, for dusting

EMPANADA FILLING

1 tsp olive oil

⅓ cup/50g diced onion

6 oz/170g small florets cauliflower or riced cauliflower

2–3 Tbsp water

1 tsp grated ginger

1 tsp minced garlic

½ tsp ground coriander seed

½ tsp ground cumin

½ tsp garam masala

⅓ tsp salt

¼ cup/40g frozen green peas

½ cup/56g grated Cheddar cheese

(continued opposite)

16g fat
144 kcal

7g protein
28 kcal

220
CALORIES
PER SERVING

12g carbs
(2g fiber)
48 kcal

Empanadas with Chimichurri

SERVES: 8

The empanada was instantly recognizable to me—similar in spirit to a samosa, and in appearance to an Indian dessert called somas (or karchikai, or karanji, or gujiya). The tangy chimichurri is of Argentinian and Uruguayan origin, but my recipe is a takeaway from our trip to Rio, where we couldn't get a lot of vegetarian local food but often ate this delicious sauce with bread. I take a few liberties here, stuffing the empanada with a samosa-esque filling, and using a blend of herbs in the chimichurri that is usually made with parsley. The versatile pastry dough can be used for pies (bake for 5 minutes longer). Leftover chimichurri can be mixed into cauliflower rice for a delicious meal the next day. Note that this recipe is a labor of love and not for someone in a hurry!

Step 1. To make the dough, combine the chickpea flour and salt in the bowl of a food processor and pulse 4–5 times until incorporated. Slice the cold butter (it must be cold; freeze for 10 minutes if necessary) into cubes and add to the food processor. Pulse for 10–15 seconds, or until you see pea-size crumbs of dough form. Add the vinegar and beaten egg and pulse for 5–10 seconds, or until it forms a sticky dough. Roll the dough into a ball, cover with plastic wrap, and refrigerate for at least 2 hours or overnight.

Step 2. For the filling, heat the oil in a medium sauté pan over medium heat and, when hot, add the onions. Cook until the onions are soft, about 5 minutes. Add the cauliflower, water, ginger, garlic, coriander, cumin, garam masala, and salt and cook, covered, until the cauliflower is tender, 10–15 minutes. Add the peas and cook until defrosted. Add the cheese, turn off the stove, and mix until the cheese has melted.

Step 3. Preheat the oven to 350°F/180°C.

Step 4. Dust a piece of parchment paper with cornstarch. Divide the dough into 4 pieces. Place one piece on the parchment and refrigerate the remaining dough until ready to use. Place another piece of parchment on top and, using a rolling pin, roll the dough into a flat tortilla of about 1/16 in/2mm thick. Using a cookie cutter

1 egg yolk, lightly beaten, for egg wash

CHIMICHURRI SAUCE

3 Tbsp olive oil

1 ½ Tbsp red wine vinegar

1 ½ tsp lemon juice

¼ cup/8g finely chopped fresh Italian parsley

3 Tbsp finely chopped cilantro/fresh coriander

1 Tbsp finely chopped mint

1 small clove garlic, minced

½ tsp dried oregano

¼ tsp fine sea salt

⅛ tsp red chile flakes

or the rim of a cup, press down on the dough to cut out 4 in/10cm discs. You will get 2–3 discs from each piece of dough. You can collect the scraps into a ball and roll it out again to get more discs.

Step 5. Spoon one heaping tablespoon of filling onto one half of each dough circle and pinch the filling into an oval shape to make empanadas easier to fold. Brush the edges of each circle with water to help bind and gently fold the other half over the filling, pressing down with your fingers to bind the edges together. Use a fork dipped in cornstarch to press down gently on the edges to create markings as pictured on page 145. Transfer to a baking sheet lined with parchment paper.

Step 6. Repeat Steps 4 and 5 with the remaining dough and filling, keeping the unused dough refrigerated (cold dough is much easier to work with). You will get 8–10 empanadas in total.

Step 7. Brush the empanadas with the egg yolk and bake for 12 minutes, or until light golden brown and the edges are crisp.

Step 8. Mix together all the ingredients for the chimichurri sauce. Serve the empanadas and chimichurri sauce together.

COOKING NOTES

Chimichurri can be made ahead and refrigerated for up to a week. Let sit at room temperature for 1 hour prior to serving.

MASALA PEANUTS

2 Tbsp chickpea flour

4 tsp water

2 tsp avocado oil, or other neutral oil of choice

2 tsp paprika

½ tsp ground turmeric

½ tsp ground cumin

½ tsp salt

½ tsp cracked black pepper

½ cup/56g raw or roasted unsalted peanuts or cashews

10 oz/280g mini sweet peppers/ capsicums (8–10 peppers), halved lengthwise with stem intact and seeded

CHILE-GARLIC MUSHROOMS

2 tsp olive oil

8 oz/225g white mushrooms, finely diced or blitzed in a food processor

2 tsp minced garlic

¾ tsp fine sea salt

¼ tsp red chile flakes

1 cup/112g goat cheese, crumbled

1 Tbsp chopped cilantro/fresh coriander

(Over)Stuffed Mini Peppers

SERVES: 8

These mini peppers started out modestly, filled with just the masala peanuts and cheese. Then, of course, I decided to make another filling with mushrooms and overstuff them. Definitely the right call. They make a hearty appetizer and will be much loved at any party!

Step 1. Preheat the air fryer to 350°F/180°C or oven to 400°F/200°C.

Step 2. Mix together the chickpea flour, water, oil, paprika, turmeric, cumin, salt, and black pepper in a bowl to make a thick marinade. Add the peanuts and mix. Try to ensure that all the peanuts get coated with the paste. Lightly spray the air fryer base with oil and spread the nut mixture evenly on the base, or spread the nuts on a parchment-lined baking sheet (you can also lightly spray the parchment). Air fry for 5 minutes, tossing halfway through, or bake for 12–15 minutes, turning over halfway through (you may need to use a spoon to scrape the peanut mixture off the parchment), until golden brown. Remove from the air fryer or oven and let cool (leave the air fryer or oven on). The nut mixture will stick together. Once cool, finely chop or pulse 3–4 times in a food processor and set aside.

Step 3. Place the mini peppers on the air fryer base or spread on a baking sheet. Spray lightly with oil if desired, and air fry for 5–6 minutes or bake for 10–12 minutes, flipping halfway through, until the peppers are soft. Let cool until you can hold them, about 5 minutes.

Step 4. Meanwhile, for the chile-garlic mushrooms, heat a medium skillet over medium heat. When hot, add the olive oil, mushrooms, garlic, salt, and chile flakes and cook, stirring occasionally, until the mushrooms are tender, about 5 minutes.

Step 5. Combine the peanuts with the crumbled goat cheese. Stuff each mini pepper with the mushrooms, then top with the peanut-goat cheese mixture (press the mixture down; you want to overstuff these!). Garnish with the cilantro and serve immediately.

10g fat
90 kcal

6g protein
24 kcal

134 CALORIES PER SERVING

5g carbs (2g fiber)
20 kcal

RISOTTO

1 tsp olive oil

12 oz/340g cauliflower rice

½ cup/120ml low-sodium vegetable broth

¼ cup/28g grated Parmesan cheese

1 large clove garlic, minced

½ tsp fine sea salt

½ tsp cracked black pepper

¼ cup/28g full-fat cream cheese

MARINARA SAUCE

1 Tbsp olive oil

¼ cup/40g diced onion

1 Tbsp minced garlic

1 (15-oz/400-g) can diced tomatoes, ideally fire-roasted

¼ tsp fine sea salt

1 tsp dried oregano

½ cup/56g diced fresh mozzarella, cut into ⅓ inch/1-cm pieces

4 oz/110g breadcrumbs from **Vegan Zucchini Bread** (page 14)

TO VEGANIZE

Use nutritional yeast in place of the Parmesan (you may need to add more salt) and use vegan cream cheese. You can use vegan mozzarella, or simply skip it.

9g fat
81 kcal

149
CALORIES
PER SERVING

7g protein
28 kcal

10g carbs
(2g fiber)
40 kcal

Arancini with Marinara

SERVES: 6   *makes 12 arancini*

Arancini are little risotto balls stuffed with mozzarella, coated with breadcrumbs, and fried. This healthy but ridiculously delicious version uses a cauliflower rice risotto coated with breadcrumbs made from my zucchini bread. The risotto should be made a day or two in advance and stored in the refrigerator, and you can make the marinara sauce ahead as well.

Step 1. To make the risotto, heat a medium sauté pan over medium heat. When hot, add the oil and cauliflower rice and cook, stirring, until the rice is dry, 10–15 minutes. Add the broth, Parmesan, garlic, salt, and pepper and mix well. Simmer until the broth is reduced and the risotto is very thick, 4–5 minutes. It is important that the risotto is not watery so it will be easy to shape into balls in Step 4. Stir in the cream cheese, cool, and refrigerate overnight or for up to 2 days.

Step 2. To make the marinara, heat a medium saucepan over medium-high heat. When hot, add the oil and onions and cook, stirring occasionally, until the onions are lightly browned, about 5 minutes. Add the garlic and cook for 30 seconds. Add the tomatoes and salt, bring to a boil, and simmer until the tomatoes break down and the sauce is reduced and thick, 10–15 minutes. Turn off the stove and stir in the oregano. Pulse a couple of times with an immersion blender, but retain some chunky texture.

Step 3. Preheat an air fryer to 400°F/200°C and spray the base lightly with oil, or preheat the oven to 450°F/225°C and line a baking sheet with parchment paper. Spread the breadcrumbs on a plate or baking sheet.

Step 4. For each arancini, make a 1½ in/4 cm diameter ball of risotto and poke a hole in the center with your finger. Stuff the ball with 3–4 pieces of mozzarella and redistribute the risotto to close up the ball (yes, it will get messy, but that's the fun of it!). Roll the ball in the breadcrumbs to coat and place in the air fryer or on the prepared baking sheet. Repeat to make 12 arancini.

Step 5. Air fry for 13–15 minutes or bake for 20–25 minutes, until deep golden brown. Serve the arancini with one-third of the marinara for dipping, and refrigerate the rest of the marinara to use as a pasta sauce.

¾ cup/90g chana dal (split chickpeas), soaked for 3 hours, rinsed, and drained

2–3 dried red Indian chiles, or 1–2 green chiles or jalapeño peppers

⅓ in/1cm piece fresh ginger

½ tsp salt

3 Tbsp avocado oil or other neutral oil of choice

⅓ cup/60g finely diced onion

3 Tbsp finely chopped cilantro/fresh coriander or fresh mint

1–2 Tbsp chickpea flour, as needed

Hot sauce or chutney, for serving

Masala Vada

SERVES: 4   *makes 12–14 vadas*

Which came first, the falafel or the masala vada? Hard to know, but these crispy fritters from South India resemble falafel both in preparation and taste (and usually have my vote!). I converted my mother-in-law's delicious recipe (traditionally deep-fried) to an air-fried or baked version that retains the crunchy texture by mixing in the oil with the batter.

Step 1. Preheat the air fryer to 400°F/200°C or oven to 450°F/230°C.

Step 2. Set aside 2 tablespoons of chana dal and reserve for later. Transfer the remaining chana dal to a small food processor and add the chile, ginger, and salt. Pulse to a coarse mixture, adding 1 tablespoon of water if needed. The mixture should resemble large grains of sand. Add the oil and the remaining 2 tablespoons chana dal to the food processor and pulse 2–3 times to combine (I like to retain some whole pieces for a crunchy bite). Transfer to a bowl.

Step 3. Add the onion and cilantro to the ground dal mixture and mix. The mixture should be wet but not watery; you should be able to shape it with your hands into a ball that doesn't break apart. If it is too watery or hard to shape, add up to 2 tablespoons chickpea flour to help it bind together.

Step 4. Shape the mixture into 1½ in/3 ¾-cm-diameter balls with your hands and flatten slightly with your palms. Place gently in a single layer on air fryer base or baking sheet (you might need to do this in two batches depending on the size of your air fryer).

Step 5. Air fry for 13–15 minutes undisturbed, checking at 13 minutes, or bake for 20–25 minutes, turning halfway through, until deep golden brown. (Oven-baked vadas may not brown as evenly, but will still taste great.) Serve with your favorite hot sauce or chutney.

12g fat
108 kcal

184
CALORIES
PER SERVING

4g protein
16 kcal

15g carbs
(4g fiber)
60 kcal

2 oz/56g spiralized daikon radish/mooli (spaghetti-size) or other veggie noodles of choice

PEANUT DIPPING SAUCE

2 Tbsp peanut butter, no sugar or additional oil added

2 tsp chile garlic sauce, such as Huy Fong

1 tsp tamari, or 2 tsp soy sauce

1 tsp store-bought tamarind concentrate paste, such as Tamicon, or 2 tsp fresh tamarind paste (page 184)

1 tsp maple syrup

2–3 Tbsp hot water, plus more as needed

1 large cucumber (11 oz/300g)

½ avocado (4 oz/100g), mashed

½ cup/40g matchstick-sliced or shredded carrots

½ cup/75g matchstick-sliced bell pepper/capsicum (any color or a mix)

½ cup/35g shredded purple cabbage

½ cup/15g fresh chopped spinach

3 Tbsp chopped cilantro/fresh coriander

Cucumber Summer Rolls

SERVES: 5   *makes 10 rolls*

A fresh take on Vietnamese summer rolls, this recipe uses thin slices of cucumber to make crunchy roll wrappers that get stuffed with a rainbow of vegetables and avocado and dipped in a spicy peanut sauce. Noodles made of daikon radish (mooli) stand in seamlessly for rice noodles. This is a fun DIY appetizer that you can make together with your guests to kick-start a party!

Step 1. Bring a pot of salted water to a boil and add the radish noodles. Cook until tender, about 5 minutes. Drain and rinse with cold water (skip this step if using zucchini noodles).

Step 2. Combine the peanut butter, chile-garlic sauce, tamari, tamarind, and maple syrup. Add the hot water, 1 tablespoon at a time as needed, and whisk together until smooth. Set aside.

Step 3. Slice the cucumber lengthwise into ¹⁄₁₆ in/2mm thick slices using a knife, peeler, or mandoline slicer (please be very careful using a mandoline; always use cut-resistant gloves). I usually get about 10 slices. Optionally divide all the toppings into 10 equal portions, or just eyeball it!

Step 4. Starting from one end as pictured, spoon a bit of the mashed avocado onto each cucumber slice and spread it a little. Place a small amount of the noodles, carrots, peppers, cabbage, spinach, and cilantro on top of the avocado. Holding them down with your fingers to pack them together, roll up the cucumber slice into a tight spiral and use a toothpick to hold it together. Repeat with the rest of the cucumber and filling ingredients.

Step 5. Serve the summer rolls with the dipping sauce.

COOKING NOTES

The sauce will thicken as it cools. Warm it up in the microwave for a few seconds before serving, or add a little bit of hot water and mix.

6g fat
54 kcal

3g protein
12 kcal

130
CALORIES
PER SERVING

16g carbs
(3g fiber)
64 kcal

BATTER FOR BREADING

¼ cup/30g chickpea flour

3 Tbsp warm water

1 tsp avocado oil or other neutral oil

¼ tsp salt

¼ tsp dried oregano

1 medium zucchini/courgette (7 oz/200g)

Salt, for sprinkling

½ cup/56g grated Parmesan cheese

LEMON AIOLI

¼ cup/55g whole-milk plain Greek yogurt

1 tsp lemon zest

1 tsp lemon juice

1 small clove garlic, minced

¼ tsp fine sea salt

¼ tsp cracked black pepper

1 Tbsp finely chopped fresh Italian parsley, for garnish

TO VEGANIZE

Replace the Parmesan with nutritional yeast and a sprinkle of salt.

Zucchini Chips

SERVES: 4

Adding Parmesan to a recipe is usually a good idea, and this dish is no exception. Brush the zucchini slices with a chickpea flour batter, sprinkle with Parmesan, and bake until crisp. The cheese is balanced by a refreshing lemon aioli that you will make over and over. This recipe was inspired by a pile of zucchini chips I had at the restaurant Nick and Toni's in the Hamptons.

Step 1. Whisk together all the ingredients for the batter and allow to sit for 1 hour.

Step 2. Slice the zucchini about ⅟₃₂ in/1mm thick using a mandoline slicer or knife. (Be very careful if using a mandoline slicer; always use cut-resistant gloves.) Sprinkle the zucchini with salt and allow to sit in a colander set over a bowl for 10–15 minutes to draw out the moisture. Pat dry with a paper towel.

Step 3. When the batter is done resting, preheat the oven to 450°F/230°C or an air fryer to 400°F/200°C.

Step 4. Lay the zucchini in a single layer on a baking sheet lined with parchment paper or the base of the air fryer. (If using an air fryer, you will need to work in batches.) Brush the batter lightly over the top of each zucchini slice and sprinkle with Parmesan.

Step 5. Bake for 9–12 minutes, until lightly browned and crisp (a few may get charred in spots). If using the air fryer, air fry for 6–7 minutes, pausing halfway to toss and gently separate the slices if necessary.

Step 6. Meanwhile, whisk together all the ingredients for the lemon aioli.

Step 7. Garnish the zucchini chips with the parsley and serve together with the lemon aioli.

COOKING NOTES

It is important that the zucchini slices are very thin, so they crisp up in the oven.

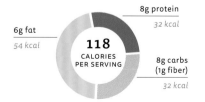

8g protein
32 kcal

6g fat
54 kcal

118
CALORIES
PER SERVING

8g carbs
(1g fiber)
32 kcal

1½ Tbsp avocado oil or other neutral oil

1½ tsp paprika

¾ tsp salt

¾ tsp ground cumin

1 large celeriac/celery root (14 oz/400g), peeled and diced into ¾ in/2-cm cubes

SMOKED PAPRIKA YOGURT SAUCE

¼ cup/55g whole-milk plain Greek yogurt

1–2 Tbsp water, as needed

½ tsp smoked paprika

¼ tsp salt

TO VEGANIZE
Use your preferred vegan yogurt for the yogurt sauce.

Celeriac Patatas Bravas

SERVES: 4

Patatas bravas always take me back to a fun evening in Ibiza with our friends when we ordered three different kinds of potato dishes from a sidewalk café (I don't remember the rationale—we were in Ibiza, after all!). Here I use celeriac or celery root as a low-carb stand in for potato. But the dish is really all about the spices, so I hope you enjoy the flavors! You can also squeeze a lemon on top for some bright acidity.

Step 1. Preheat the air fryer to 400°F/200°C or oven to 450°F/230°C.

Step 2. Mix the oil, paprika, salt, and cumin in a bowl to make the marinade. Add the diced celeriac to the marinade and mix well to coat all the pieces.

Step 3. Air fry for 8–10 minutes or bake (on a baking sheet lined with parchment paper) for 13–15 minutes, tossing halfway through, until deep golden brown on the outside.

Step 4. Mix together all the ingredients for the sauce. Drizzle the sauce over the celeriac and serve.

COOKING NOTES

Note that these will not get as crispy as potatoes, as their starch content is much lower.

You could also try this with jicama or daikon radish (mooli) if you cannot source celeriac.

3g protein
12 kcal

6g fat
54 kcal

106
CALORIES PER SERVING

10g carbs (2g fiber)
40 kcal

1 medium jicama (1 lb/450g), sliced into matchsticks ¼ in/6mm wide and 2 in/5cm long

1 Tbsp avocado oil or other neutral oil

1 tsp garlic powder

1 tsp paprika

½ tsp salt

⅛ tsp cayenne

LEMON AIOLI

¼ cup/55g whole-milk plain Greek yogurt

1 tsp lemon zest

1 tsp lemon juice

1 small clove garlic, minced

¼ tsp fine sea salt

¼ tsp cracked black pepper

TO VEGANIZE
Use your preferred vegan yogurt for the lemon aioli.

Jicama French Fries

SERVES: 2

I have tried everything to create a low-carb version of French fries, using celery root and even radish, but jicama comes closest to mimicking the texture of the real thing due to its slightly higher starch content. They're still not potatoes, I know, but these fries are solid, especially together with the lemon aioli!

Step 1. Bring a pot of salted water to a boil. Cook the jicama until fork-tender, 10–15 minutes. Drain and rinse with cold water and pat dry.

Step 2. Preheat the air fryer to 400°F/200°C or oven to 450°F/230°C.

Step 3. Mix together the oil, garlic powder, paprika, salt, and cayenne in a large bowl to make the marinade. Add the jicama and toss to coat.

Step 4. If using an air fryer, spray the base lightly with oil. Spread the jicama in a single layer (you may need to work in two to three batches depending on the size of your air fryer). Air fry for 8–10 minutes, tossing 2–3 times. If using the oven, spread the jicama evenly on a baking sheet lined with parchment paper. Bake for 15–20 minutes, turning the fries over halfway through and spraying them lightly with oil, until crispy and golden brown on the outside.

Step 5. Meanwhile, mix together all the ingredients for the lemon aioli. Season the fries with additional salt and pepper and serve with the aioli.

COOKING NOTES

If jicama is not available, you could also use radish or celeriac. However, they will be a bit softer.

9g fat
81 kcal

181
CALORIES
PER SERVING

4g protein
16 kcal

21g carbs
(11g fiber)
84 kcal

SMOOTHIES

I do love me a good smoothie, especially on days when it feels like too much work to chew. But the norm in today's smoothie culture is little sugar bombs that masquerade as healthy options. While it's still possible to create a fruit smoothie that is good for you, in this book I challenge you to try a little something different—a savory smoothie!

Once again, I've drawn inspiration from cultural traditions around the world. We start with the Indian **lassi** (page 165), travel to Spain for two versions of **gazpacho** (page 166), get a little kick out of a spicy margarita-inspired **Avocado Lime Smoothie** (page 169), and then head back to India to finish with a refreshing **Masala Chaas** (page 170).

These recipes are extremely versatile and can be consumed as a drink, cold soups, or . . . wait for it . . . salad dressings! I've even been known to do a shot or two of my gazpacho smoothies on a hot summer afternoon.

1 cup/220g whole-milk plain Greek yogurt

2–4 Tbsp water, as needed

2 Tbsp dry-roasted unsalted almonds

2 small green Indian chiles, jalapeño peppers, or Thai chiles

1 Tbsp water

2 tsp grated ginger

½ tsp ground turmeric

½ tsp salt

TO VEGANIZE
Use your favorite plant-based yogurt in place of the whole-milk Greek yogurt.

Turmeric-Almond Lassi

SERVES: 2

Lassi is a blended Punjabi yogurt drink that usually comes in a salted or sweet version. This is my spicy take on the salt lassi version, and adds on turmeric and almonds for extra goodness. Frothy and refreshing, it is the O.G. savory smoothie!

Step 1. Combine all the ingredients in a blender and blend until smooth. Add more water as needed to reach the desired consistency. Serve chilled.

11g protein
44 kcal

9g fat
81 kcal

149
CALORIES
PER SERVING

6g carbs
(1g fiber)
24 kcal

TOMATO GAZPACHO

1½ cups/225g ripe cherry tomatoes (or 2–3 ripe Roma tomatoes, quartered)

1 cup/220g whole-milk plain Greek yogurt

1 Tbsp water, plus more as needed

1 Tbsp red wine vinegar

1 tsp olive oil

½ tsp minced garlic

¾ tsp fine sea salt

½ tsp smoked paprika

CUCUMBER MINT GAZPACHO

1 large cucumber (11 oz/300g), peeled and roughly chopped

1 cup/220g whole-milk Greek yogurt

1 small clove garlic, minced

6–8 fresh mint leaves

1 Tbsp water, plus more as needed

1 Tbsp lemon juice

1 tsp olive oil

½ tsp fine sea salt

½ tsp ground cumin

TO VEGANIZE
Use your favorite plant-based yogurt in place of the whole-milk Greek yogurt.

Gazpacho Smoothies

SERVES: 2   *per smoothie*

There is nothing quite as refreshing to the palate on a hot summer day as gazpacho. A traditional cold soup from Spain, it is typically made from raw blended vegetables, garlic, wine vinegar, and olive oil. Tomato gazpacho is possibly the most popular version. Add Greek yogurt and you have an instant protein boost that keeps the deep tomato flavor. Be sure to chill this one for at least 4 hours, or ideally overnight.

The green gazpacho with cucumber and mint, meanwhile, is another summery option that's reminiscent of raita or tzatziki. If you'd like to serve these as soups instead of as smoothies, you can garnish them with chives or parsley.

Step 1. Combine all the ingredients for the tomato gazpacho or the cucumber mint gazpacho in a blender, add 1 tablespoon of water, and blend until smooth. Add more water as needed to reach the desired consistency.

Step 2. Chill for 4–6 hours prior to serving.

TOMATO GAZPACHO

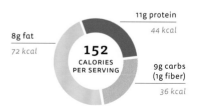

8g fat
72 kcal

11g protein
44 kcal

152 CALORIES PER SERVING

9g carbs (1g fiber)
36 kcal

CUCUMBER MINT GAZPACHO

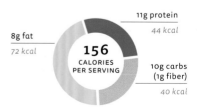

8g fat
72 kcal

11g protein
44 kcal

156 CALORIES PER SERVING

10g carbs (1g fiber)
40 kcal

1 medium avocado (7 oz/200g), scooped

1½ cups/330g whole-milk Greek yogurt

1 small jalapeño pepper, roughly chopped

¼ cup/4g chopped cilantro/fresh coriander

2 Tbsp lime juice

1 tsp ground cumin

¾ tsp fine sea salt

4–8 Tbsp/60–120ml water, as needed

TO VEGANIZE
Use your favorite plant-based yogurt in place of the whole-milk Greek yogurt.

Avocado Lime Smoothie

SERVES: 2

While the ingredients for this smoothie may resemble guacamole in a glass, I believe it was subconsciously inspired by the flavor of spicy margaritas! Pair with the **Burrito Jar** (page 57) for a little feast, or use as salad dressing. Only make as much as you can use at one time, as the avocado will not keep well.

Step 1. Combine the avocado, yogurt, jalapeño, cilantro, lime juice, cumin, salt, and ¼ cup/60ml of water, and blend until smooth. Add more water or ice as needed to reach the desired consistency. Serve chilled.

COOKING NOTES

For a less-spicy smoothie, remove the seeds from the jalapeño pepper. Leave the seeds in if you prefer a bit of heat.

17g protein
68 kcal

23g fat
207 kcal

343
CALORIES
PER SERVING

17g carbs
(7g fiber)
68 kcal

2 cups/480ml whole-milk buttermilk, kefir, or diluted yogurt

12–15 fresh mint leaves

½ tsp ground cumin

½ tsp fine sea salt

½ tsp cracked black pepper

⅓ tsp asafoetida (hing, sometimes called yellow powder)

TO VEGANIZE
Use your favorite plant-based yogurt in place of the whole-milk kefir or buttermilk.

Masala Chaas

SERVES: 2

This lightly spiced buttermilk drink is called chaas in North India and moru in South India, and is often consumed as part of a meal to help with digestion. I've found that kefir also works really well in this recipe and I often use it when I can't find full-fat buttermilk. Light and refreshing, this makes a great thirst quencher on hot summer afternoons!

Step 1. Combine all the ingredients in a blender and blend until smooth. Serve chilled.

8g protein
32 kcal

8g fat
72 kcal

156
CALORIES
PER SERVING

13g carbs
(3g fiber)
52 kcal

DESSERTS

This dessert chapter was not part of my original plan for this book. But when I stalled out on creating smoothies, I decided to try dessert instead. In the end it turned out to be the part of the book that I had the most fun creating! I have been baking for a couple of decades now, but the challenge of creating naturally sweetened desserts was unique.

I use whole fruit to sweeten all desserts in this book, and you will find them lightly sweet but craveable and satiating.

Chocoholics, I point you in the direction of the **Hazelnut Brownie** (page 175). For berry lovers like myself, I created the stunning **Berry Cashew Burfi** (page 176). If you need a little pick-me-up with your afternoon tea, look no further than my **PB&J Sandwich Cookies** (page 180). And for more filling tropical options (that are okay to have for breakfast!) try my **Banana Soufflé** or **Mango Cheesecake Jars** (pages 179 and 183). There is a little something for everyone in this section that you can reach for, guilt-free.

15–20 pitted mejdool dates
(12 oz/340g)

1 cup/240ml hot water

4 eggs, beaten

1 cup/224g hazelnut butter or other
nut butter (no sugar or additional oil
added)

1 tsp vanilla extract

1 cup/112g blanched almond flour

1 cup/86g unsweetened cocoa
powder (I use Valrhona for an intense
dark color)

1 tsp baking powder

¼ tsp salt

Hazelnut Brownies

SERVES: 16   *makes 16 brownies*

I like my brownies so fudgy you need to eat them with a spoon, if
you know what I'm saying. These rich, gooey brownies have a hint of
hazelnut reminiscent of Nutella and are sweetened only with dates.

If you can get your hands on unsweetened hazelnut butter or
make your own, it will be an absolute treat, but you can sub in any
unsweetened nut butter for great results. This one is a classic that you
will make over and over.

Step 1. Immerse the dates in hot water, cover, and let sit, for
10–15 minutes. Drain and reserve the water. In the carafe of a food
processor or blender, blend the dates with ½ cup/120ml of the
reserved water until smooth. You can add more water from the
remaining reserved water as needed, 1 tablespoon at a time.

Step 2. Preheat the oven to 350°F/180°C.

Step 3. In a large bowl, whisk together the beaten eggs, hazelnut
butter, vanilla extract, and date paste until smooth. In a separate
bowl, mix the flour, cocoa, baking powder, and salt.

Step 4. Add the dry ingredients to the wet ingredients gradually,
mixing well until fully incorporated.

Step 5. Grease an 8-x-8-x-1 ½ in/20-x-20-x-4-cm baking pan or
casserole dish and pour in the batter. Bake for 18–22 minutes (see
cooking notes).

Step 6. Let cool for 30 minutes. Slice into 16 rectangles and serve.
You may need to run a butter knife around the edges to loosen.

COOKING NOTES

For a fudgy brownie that you need to eat with a spoon, bake for
18–20 minutes. Bake for 20–22 minutes for a brownie you can hold.

Halve the recipe for an 8½-x-4½-x-2½ inch/21-x-11-x-6-cm loaf pan.
These freeze beautifully, too! You can freeze the whole slab or cut it
in half. Wrapped in plastic wrap, the baked brownies will keep for up
to 3 months in the freezer.

The date paste keeps well in the fridge for about 10 days and in the
freezer for up to 3 months.

14g fat
126 kcal

7g protein
28 kcal

246
CALORIES
PER SERVING

23g carbs
(6g fiber)
92 kcal

1 tsp cornstarch/cornflour

1 tsp water

2 cups/300g hulled ripe strawberries, pureed until smooth

2 cups/300g ripe blueberries, pureed until smooth (use frozen berries if berries are not in season)

1 tsp lemon juice

2 Tbsp maple syrup

10 oz/280g raw cashews, blanched almonds, or pistachios

1½ tsp ghee, divided

Edible silver foil (sheet size varies; enough to cover a 9-x-9 inch/23-x-23-cm area; optional)

TO VEGANIZE
Replace the ghee with any neutral oil such as avocado oil.

Berry Cashew Burfi

SERVES: 10   *makes about 30 pieces*

Cashew burfi (also known as kaju katli) is a diamond-shaped fudge with an edible silver-leaf topping that is probably the most gifted Diwali sweet in India! This fabulously purple version is naturally sweetened with strawberries, blueberries, and a little maple syrup. Lightly sweet with a touch of tartness from the berries, this is my favorite of the desserts in this book.

Step 1. Stir the cornstarch and water together in a bowl to make a slurry. Mix the slurry, strawberry and blueberry purees, lemon juice, and maple syrup together in a large nonstick pan. Bring to a boil over medium-high heat and cook, stirring often and scraping down the pan until very thick, jam-like, and reduced to a quarter of the original volume as the water evaporates, 15–20 minutes.

Step 2. Place the cashews in a food processor and process until powdered.

Step 3. When the berry mixture is done cooking, turn off the heat and add the powdered cashews, pressing down with a spatula if necessary, until well incorporated. The mixture will leave the sides of the pan and become a sticky dough ball, about the consistency of clay. If it's still wet and loose, let it cook a little more in the pan on medium heat until it thickens. Let cool for 10 minutes.

Step 4. Line a flat surface with wax paper. Grease your palms with ½ teaspoon of ghee and transfer the dough ball to the wax paper. Place another sheet of wax paper on top. Using a rolling pin, roll out a square(ish) slab, approximately 9 x 9 in/23 x 23cm and ⅓ in/8mm thick.

Step 5. If using the silver foil, remove the upper wax paper and brush the top of the burfi slab with the remaining 1 teaspoon of ghee. Carefully place the edible silver foil on top (allow it to fall rather than placing it with your hands so that it doesn't tear too much), covering as much of the slab as possible.

Step 6. Freeze for 30–40 minutes or until set. Slice the burfi into rhombus shapes (2 in/5cm sides) with a sharp knife and serve.

COOKING NOTES

Store in an airtight container, with layers separated by wax paper in the fridge, for up to 2 weeks, or in the freezer for up to 3 months.

13g fat
117 kcal

6g protein
24 kcal

213
CALORIES
PER SERVING

18g carbs
(2g fiber)
72 kcal

1 cup/150g mashed ripe banana
(from 2 medium bananas)

¼ cup/64g peanut butter or almond
butter (with no sugar or additional
oil added)

½ tsp vanilla extract

2 egg yolks, lightly beaten

3 egg whites

Tiny pinch of salt

Banana Soufflés

SERVES: 4

This recipe elevates an old microwave mug-cake recipe to an art
form and will be your new go-to for overripe bananas. Moist from
the banana, airy from the beaten egg whites, yet filling from the nut
butter, this is a healthy dessert that feels luxurious. Soufflés are best
served immediately, so prep the mixture in ramekins and store in
the refrigerator until ready to pop them in the oven.

Step 1. Preheat the oven to 400°F/200°C. Grease four 4-oz/112g
ramekins thoroughly (including the rim) with butter and put them
in the freezer to set. You can also use any oven-safe cups if you don't
have ramekins.

Step 2. Blend the banana, peanut butter, and vanilla extract together
in a food processor or blender until smooth. Stir in the egg yolks with
a spatula and mix well.

Step 3. In the bowl of a stand mixer fitted with the whisk attachment,
beat the egg whites at low speed for 2–3 minutes. (Or beat by hand
in a bowl using a balloon whisk.) Add the salt and continue to beat
at medium speed until the egg white forms glossy, firm peaks (egg
white at the top of the whisk does not droop when you pull away),
5–8 minutes.

Step 4. In a separate bowl, combine the banana–peanut butter
mixture with a third of the egg whites and use a spatula to mix until
well incorporated. This will lighten up the base. Pour the lightened
base over the remaining egg whites and fold the mixture gently
with the spatula, making circular motions that go along the bottom
of the bowl under the whites and then flip over the top, until the
whites are just incorporated.

Step 5. Remove the ramekins from the freezer. Spoon the mixture
into the ramekins until 1 in/2.5cm from the top. Tap on the counter
to settle. Add more of the mixture to fill each ramekin completely,
and flatten out the tops with a butter knife. Run your thumb around
the rim to separate the mixture from the sides.

Step 6. Bake for 12–14 minutes, or until the soufflés rise and are
golden brown. Serve immediately.

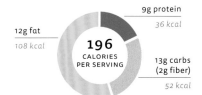

9g protein
36 kcal

12g fat
108 kcal

196
CALORIES
PER SERVING

13g carbs
(2g fiber)
52 kcal

GRAPE JELLY

1 tsp cornstarch/cornflour

1 tsp water

12 oz/340g seedless red or green grapes, pureed until smooth

COOKIE DOUGH

1 cup/112g blanched almond flour

½ cup/45g gluten-free rolled oats, powdered in a food processor (OK if a bit coarse)

2 oz/56g butter, melted and cooled

2 Tbsp maple syrup

1 tsp vanilla extract

1 tsp cornstarch/cornflour, for dusting

¼ cup/64g peanut butter, no sugar or additional oil added

> ## TO VEGANIZE
> Use coconut oil in place of the butter (try to use one that has very little taste or aroma).

PB&J Sandwich Cookies

SERVES: 8   *makes 8 cookie sandwiches*

These flaky almond flour shortbread-style cookies will quickly become a staple in your pantry. Here I make them extra sumptuous by creating a cookie sandwich with peanut butter and a two ingredient grape jelly (so easy!). Don't like grape jelly? Just make strawberry or blueberry jelly instead. You can also use ricotta or cream cheese in place of the peanut butter.

Step 1. To make the grape jelly, stir the cornstarch and water together in a bowl to make a slurry. Combine the grape puree with the cornstarch slurry in a nonstick pan over medium-high heat and cook, stirring often, until the mixture is reduced to a quarter of the original volume and is the consistency of a very thick jam, 20–25 minutes. Let cool.

Step 2. Preheat the oven to 350°F/180°C.

Step 3. To make the cookie dough, combine the almond flour and powdered oats in a bowl. Add the butter, maple syrup, and vanilla extract. Mix first with a spoon, then knead a little with your hands to form a lightly sticky ball of dough, the texture of clay. Refrigerate for 15 minutes.

Step 4. Dust a sheet of parchment paper with cornstarch and roll out the dough to a roughly 8-x-8 in/20-x-20-cm square about ⅛ in/3mm thick. (I often use a cake pan, line it with parchment, and pat the dough out to the correct dimensions inside the pan, then remove the parchment with the dough and continue with the remaining steps.) The dough can be a bit crumbly but it is forgiving, and you can easily press it back into place or redistribute as necessary.

Step 5. Using a knife greased with oil or butter, slice the dough into 16 squares and gently push with the knife to make a little space between each cookie on the parchment paper. Place the parchment with the cookies onto a baking sheet and bake for 12–15 minutes, or until firm and the edges are browned. Let cool completely, for 1 hour—this is really important, or the cookies will fall apart!

Step 6. Pipe or spoon 1–2 teaspoons of peanut butter on one cookie, and 1–2 teaspoons of grape jelly on another. Press the two together gently to make a sandwich. Repeat with the remaining cookies.

COOKING NOTES

Store for up to 2 weeks at room temperature in an airtight container.

17g fat
153 kcal

5g protein
20 kcal

241
CALORIES
PER SERVING

17g carbs
(3g fiber)
68 kcal

4 oz/112g full-fat cream cheese, at room temperature

4 oz/112g whole-milk ricotta cheese, at room temperature

4–6 oz/112–168g mango pulp, pureed until smooth, at room temperature

1½ tsp cornstarch/cornflour

1 tsp vanilla extract

1 egg, at room temperature

2 tsp pistachios, chopped, for garnish (optional)

Pinch of saffron, for garnish (optional)

Mango Cheesecake Jars

SERVES: 4

Here is one healthy enough to eat for breakfast and, unexpectedly, approved by my daughter! When in season, try to use a sweeter variety of mangoes for this recipe, such as Indian Kesar or Alphonso or Mexican Ataulfo. You can also use the kind that comes canned, but try to find one without added sugar. If you don't have mason jars or ramekins, use any oven-safe cups.

Step 1. Preheat the oven to 325°F/150°C. Grease four 4-oz/112-g mason jars or ramekins with butter and freeze for 10–15 minutes as you prep. This will help the cheesecake rise without sticking to the sides.

Step 2. Beat the cream cheese and ricotta together in a large bowl with an electric mixer at low speed for 2–3 minutes, scraping down the sides often, until well integrated and smooth. You can also use a blender or food processor if you don't have an electric mixer.

Step 3. Stir in 4 oz/112g of mango puree, the cornstarch, and vanilla extract and beat at low speed for 20–30 seconds to mix. Taste and add up to 2 oz/56g more mango puree if needed for sweetness, saving 2 tablespoons of puree for garnish.

Step 4. Add the egg and stir gently with a fork; do not beat. Remove the jars from the freezer and gently spoon the batter in, leaving about ⅔ in/2cm at the top for the cheesecakes to rise.

Step 5. Place the jars in a baking pan (I use an 8-x-8-x-1 ½ in/20-x-20-x-4-cm pan). Add hot water directly into the pan (not into the jars!), filling to about two-thirds the height of the jars. This water bath will help the cheesecakes bake at a lower temperature, resulting in a smoother and creamier texture.

Step 6. Bake for 20–25 minutes, or until the tops are just set.

Step 7. Remove the baking pan from the oven and let the jars cool on the counter for 1 hour or so until they reach room temperature. Refrigerate for at least 4 hours, or overnight, before serving.

Step 8. Garnish with the mango puree, pistachio, and saffron, if using, just prior to serving. Serve chilled.

COOKING NOTES

Seal the jars with lids or plastic wrap to store and refrigerate for up to 1 week or freeze for up to 1 month.

16g fat
144 kcal

208
CALORIES
PER SERVING

6g protein
24 kcal

10g carbs
(1g fiber)
40 kcal

Breadcrumbs from Vegan Zucchini Bread

Step 1. Preheat the oven to 300°F/150°C.

Step 2. Pulse 2–3 slices **Vegan Zucchini Bread** (page 14) to a coarse powder (the texture of sand) in a food processor. Spread on a baking sheet lined with parchment paper and bake for 8–10 minutes, stirring halfway through, until dry and lightly browned.

Use just as you would panko breadcrumbs!

NOTE

Store in a resealable bag at room temperature for up to 4 weeks or for up to 6 months in the freezer.

Fresh Tamarind Paste

Step 1. Immerse a golf ball–size piece of tamarind in hot water (just enough to submerge) for 20 minutes. Squeeze out the pulp using your hands, then strain the mixture by passing it through a fine-mesh sieve to make a thick paste.

COOKING NOTES

Refrigerate in an airtight container for up to 2 weeks.

2 Tbsp olive oil

3 Tbsp chickpea flour

2 cups/480ml plant-based milk of choice (unsweetened)

½ tsp salt

½ tsp cracked black pepper

Vegan Béchamel Sauce

SERVES: 4

A simple creamy white sauce spells comfort to me, whether in a mac 'n' cheese or simply to lighten up a tomato or pesto sauce. I am particularly excited about this vegan and gluten-free version that uses olive oil, chickpea flour, and the non-dairy milk of your choice. Add nutritional yeast for a cheesy flavor and protein boost!

Step 1. Heat a medium saucepan (preferably nonstick) over medium-low heat. Add the olive oil and chickpea flour and stir continuously with a spatula to blend into a paste.

Step 2. Add the milk gradually, stirring constantly to prevent lumps. Increase the heat to medium and simmer, stirring often, until thickened (about twice as thick as heavy cream/double cream), 15–20 minutes. You can turn up the heat a touch to help it along as needed.

Step 3. Add the salt and pepper and mix.

COOKING NOTES

Refrigerate in an airtight container for up to 10 days.

Get creative by adding seasonings—ground nutmeg, chile flakes, and garlic powder are all winners!

Recommended Reading

BOOKS

Bikman, Benjamin. 2020. *Why We Get Sick*. Dallas: BenBella Books, Inc.

Fung, Jason. *The Obesity Code: Unlocking the Secrets of Weight Loss (Why Intermittent Fasting Is the Key to Controlling Your Weight)*. Vancouver/Berkeley: Greystone Books

Hyman, Mark. 2012. *The Blood Sugar Solution: The UltraHealthy Program for Losing Weight, Preventing Disease and Feeling Great Now!* New York: Little, Brown Spark.

Mosley, Michael. 2020. *The Fast 800 Diet: Discover the Ideal Fasting Formula to Shed Pounds, Fight Disease, and Boost Your Overall Health*. New York: Atria Books.

Moss, Michael. 2014. *Salt Sugar Fat: How the Food Giants Hooked Us*. New York: Random House Trade Paperbacks.

Pollan, Michael. 2008. *In Defense of Food: An Eater's Manifesto*. New York: The Penguin Press.

Pollan, Michael. 2006. *The Omnivore's Dilemma*. New York: The Penguin Press.

Taubes, Gary. 2008. *Good Calories, Bad Calories: Fats, Carbs, and the Controversial Science of Diet and Health*. New York: Anchor Books.

RESEARCH

Bhardwaj, Bhaskar, Evan L. O'Keefe, and James H. O'Keefe. 2016. "Death by Carbs: Added Sugars and Refined Carbohydrates Cause Diabetes and Cardiovascular Disease in Asian Indians." *Missouri Medicine* Sept.–Oct.

Ludwig, David S., Louis J. Aronne, Arne Astrup, Rafael de Cabo, Lewis C. Cantley, Mark I. Friedman, Steven B. Heymsfield, James D. Johnson, Janet C. King, Ronald M. Krauss, Daniel E. Lieberman, Gary Taubes, Jeff S. Volek, Eric C. Westman, Walter C. Willett, William S. Yancy, Jr. and Cara B. Ebbeling. 2021. "The carbohydrate insulin model: a physiological perspective on the obesity pandemic." *The American Journal of Clinical Nutrition* vol.114 (Dec.).

Zinöcker, Marit K. and Inge A. Lindseth. 2018. "The Western Diet–Microbiome-Host Interaction and Its Role in Metabolic Disease." *Nutrients* Mar. 17.

A Note About Nutrition

The nutritional information in this book has been calculated using information from the USDA database or from ingredient nutritional panel information. Although we strive to provide accurate data, the nutritional information provided in this book or on our website should only be considered an estimate or approximation of the nutritional content of a recipe. Numerous variable factors determine the actual nutritional content in any given recipe. Examples include different product types or brands, normal fluctuations in agricultural or natural ingredients, substitutions, serving sizes, and the various ways ingredients are processed by their producers. Substitutions or variations in the ingredients used, quantities measured, or cooking techniques employed may change the nutritional information, sometimes considerably.

I am not a certified nutritionist, dietician, or medical professional. Everyone's dietary needs and restrictions are unique to that individual and I am in no way providing medical, nutritional, or dietary advice.

The book and my website may indicate that a recipe is gluten- or dairy-free. If you are following a gluten-free or dairy-free diet, please note that this is based solely on the specific preparation and exact ingredients used in the recipe development. Your own results may vary.

A Note to My Readers

I wrote this cookbook and created the "We Ate Well" community to redefine eating healthy and put nutrition back in focus for foodies like me. I hope you find the recipes in this book interesting and enjoyable. If even *one* of them makes it into the rotation for yourself and/or your family, I would love to hear from you!

Contact me via my website **v8well.com**, where you can also sign up for my newsletter. You can also join the We Ate Well community on social media using the handle **@v8well**.

I'd be so honored if you would write a review on the platform where you purchased the book, in order to help other readers find it more easily. Your feedback is important to me, and you can be sure that I will read and obsess over every single review!

Acknowledgments

This book was a labor of love that would not have been possible without my village of support.

To my dear family—my mom, dad, sister, and in-laws—your staunch support is the wind beneath my wings and gives me the confidence to keep trying. Thank you to my parents and extended family in Bangalore that always encouraged my culinary experiments growing up! The delight in your eyes when you see an interesting recipe and the quiet pride when you see my modest achievements is the fuel that keeps me going. Thank you for being in my corner as I navigate this life and career change.

To my wonderful friends—thank you for cheering me on as I venture on this path. This project has deepened my connections with so many of you as we share our love for food, cooking and entrepreneurship, and the shared excitement has made my journey so much more fun and meaningful.

To my most dedicated recipe testers from all over the world—Poojitha Rao, Adeline Ramirez, Radha and Chaitanya Y., Linda Harley Gillespie, Chris Bevan, Jennifer Hutzel, Mary Watkin and Sitara Siddraj—thank you for being there for me from the beginning and being adventurous enough to continue to try my recipes even when they bombed spectacularly. Your candid feedback has made me a better cook and a better writer. To the countless others in the Fast800 community who have tried my recipes and cheered me on from the early days of this project—I can't thank you enough. You gave me the momentum to turn this from a small side project into a finished product and I hope you all enjoy it.

To my talented A-team—Alexandra Shytsman, my photographer, Christine McKnight, my copy editor, and Liliana Guia, my designer—I benefited not only from your impeccable work that elevated the quality of my book, but also from your advice and experience. Thank you for putting up with my endless reschedules and for helping me create a high-quality experience for my readers. Thank you to Estefania Trujillo Preciado for so expertly assisting us during the fun but grueling photoshoot! Thank you to Angela Engel, Amy Treadwell, AJ Hansen, and the team at Collective Book Studio for this beautiful finished product and taking my book to market. And to Carrie Bachman, my publicist, thank you for showcasing my book to the world.

To my husband, Shyam, who has been my partner and confidante from the seeds of this project (and has suffered through my experiments!)—this would have stayed a dream without you. Your clear vision, wise counsel, brutally honest feedback paired with unconditional support and constant reassurance is the reason I can take a risk and fail, and know it will be okay. And if I succeed, it will be sweeter for having shared it with you.

Index